The Path of Remembering

Who We Are and Why We're Here

Maureen Kennedy

Transcribed by
Maureen Kennedy

Mount Hope Press

The Path of Remembering
    Who We Are and Why We're Here

Transcribed by Maureen Kennedy

Copyright © 2010 by Maureen Kennedy
Mount Hope Press
P. O. Box 214
Colrain, Massachusetts 01340

Book and cover design: Claudia Wells, bluemandalastudio.com
Cover art: Sandra Dovberg, sandracdovbergart.com

LCCN: 2010902107
ISBN: 978-0-615-35151-3

Printed in the United States of America

The criterion is always —

what would Love do?

Contents

Acknowledgments

Lee Kass, my dear friend and long-time believer in the Committee's teachings; and Stan Kass, whose scientific mind is expansive enough to hold the reality of the Committee, for their generous investment in the publication of this book.

Judy Brownell, for her most generous gifts, and most of all, for her friendship.

Judy Hyde and Helen Armstrong, who have supported me faithfully in the publication of the Committee's wisdom, both financially and emotionally.

Patricia Greene, a gifted writer, who was the first to

share my vision for this book.

Jim Ballard, Emily Johns, Susan Gleason and Dr. Paul Langman, editors extraordinaire, whose expertise and care with both the small details and big themes of the book have made an enormous difference.

Claudia Wells, designer of the book and cover, whose energy and creativity has turned hundreds of typed pages into a book whose look beautifully complements the Committee's words.

Judith Thomas-Solomon and Danai Gagné, colleagues and old friends, to whom I first dared read the Committee's transmissions. Judith and Danai have been cheerleaders along this journey, along with Chris Thomas on the west coast.

Rabbi Josef Solomon, a Renaissance thinker, who can include the possibility of the Committee along with his ancient prophetic tradition.

Barbara Gilford, friend and travel companion, who has patiently walked with me through great cathedrals and tiny Norman chapels.

Stan Pike, artist, pal and computer expert, who bails me

Acknowledgments

out of computer malfunctions and lives his life with great equanimity.

Sue Kuttner Feuerbach, cousin, Reiki master, and spiritual warrior, for her encouragement and friendship.

Peggy Hughes, impeccable grammarian, who coached me on the pitfalls of the passive voice.

Alison Crowther, who has so generously shared with me the stories of her son Welles's heroism on 9/11.

Sandra Dovberg, whose cover painting elegantly distills the book's message.

The members of my spiritual support group, for their friendship and encouragement: Margaret Boone, Linda Comstock, Leslie Fraser, Sherrill Hogen, Liz Kelner, Margaret Olin, Eve Brown-Waite, Pam Walker, and especially Sue Pratt, for her practical help and enthusiasm for the Committee's teachings.

My sons, Christopher, Justin and Stuart Kenney, for their love and support.

Introduction

Maureen's Story

On a sultry August night more than twenty years ago, I pulled into the driveway of an old bed and breakfast in a southern Vermont village. This weekend away from my demanding life in Boston was a gift from my son Stuart. It allowed me needed space from a deteriorating relationship with my partner at that time, who was a physician.

My corner room was filled with elegant early nineteenth century antiques. On the floor under the front window was a cooler containing a bottle of wine and some cheese and fruit, a welcoming present from Stuart. After my nightly ritual of reading in bed, I fell deeply asleep. Sometime during the night, I woke up to voices saying, "Get up! Get up!" I was certain I'd been dreaming. I turned over and tried to go back to sleep, but the voices persisted. "Get some paper and a pen and start writing." Next, I thought I heard chuckling and, "An apple a day keeps the doctor away!" Clearly, these voices knew me and were teasing me about my life. The room suddenly seemed crowded. At the time, I didn't know enough about mental illness to fear that I might be having a psychotic break, so I got up, climbed into an old wing chair and grabbed a yellow legal pad and pen.

What followed astonished me. Words began to flow through me that were not from my conscious mind. After a few minutes I paused and asked myself—is it possible that this is happening? Am I making it all up? Although I didn't understand, I was curious, so I continued to write and quickly filled several pages. When 'they' finally stopped dictating, I leaned back, took a deep breath, and shook out my wrist, stiff from taking so many notes. It didn't occur to me to be afraid, but I wondered why these energies, who seemed to have very real personalities, were choosing to speak to me.

From that first night, the voices began to talk about what would become their central themes:

- You are eternally loved and safe.
- Life's journey is an opportunity to remember who you are.
- You have a choice to live either in love or fear.

Over the next few weeks, I continued to think about possible explanations for this strange and recurring phenomenon. Were these voices guides from a spiritual plane? Was my higher self or soul speaking to me? Was this a part of my mind that worked in some kind of autonomic, non-linear way? Was I tuning in to the collective unconscious of which Jung speaks? Or was I having delusions that are labeled 'crazy' in our society?

That summer night was the beginning of a collaboration with those I've come to call 'the Committee.' Whenever I sit down, quiet my mind and invite them in, these 'friends' are ready to share their wisdom. Less often, I feel a kind of antsyness that I've learned to recognize as a sign that they want to talk. Their messages are sometimes personal, in response to specific questions that I or others ask, but most often they leapfrog from the personal to larger themes such as life as a journey on the Path.

In the beginning, I noticed that these voices had different styles of 'speaking.' One I nicknamed Basil. He seemed to reiterate every idea in several different ways, and had a fondness for big old-fashioned words. I imagined him as a Victorian gentleman. There was another I named Joe. He spoke in short sentences and got straight to the point. There was another voice that was poetic. Over the years, however, the voices have blended, and now I experience the Committee as speaking with one voice. I don't hear them with my ears. Rather, I 'hear' them speaking inside my head.

They dictate as fast as it's comfortable for me to write down what they say. If I'm at a keyboard, I notice that they speed up to match my typing. Rarely, and only with old and trusted friends (I think this is because of my innate shyness) do I speak out loud what the Committee says. I don't go into trance. My voice and mannerisms remain the same. And before any session with the Committee, I always say a quick prayer asking that I have access only to the highest energies.

Over the years, I notice more and more how familiar the presence of the Committee has become in my life. I've come to believe that this connection to higher truth and wisdom is available to anyone who asks for it, *and* that it can happen in unique and unexpected ways. My experience is only one way.

I filled many notebooks with the Committee's writings before I dared share them with friends and family. One summer, while I was teaching at an oceanside university, I finally found the courage to read the Committee's writings to long-time colleagues as we relaxed one evening on the beach. They loved what they heard and believed the Committee's words. Their encouragement gave me the confidence to read excerpts of these transmissions to other friends. Finally, I dared to share the Committee's writings with my sons, who I was sure would think I'd gone 'round the bend.' To my great relief, they were supportive and continue to accept the Committee's role in my life.

Everyone who has been introduced to these teachings has

urged me to get them out into the world. I know it's important to communicate that a connection to such creative and loving non-physical energy is not reserved for saints and mystics. The Committee is eager for humans to discover that it's possible for people like you and me to tap into a universal source of wisdom.

I'm learning that *we* allow an opening so that the spiritual realm can communicate with *us*. It's the opposite of traditional notions of prayer as asking and beseeching. As the Committee says a little irreverently, it's a matter of 'sitting down and shutting up.' It's like tuning in to the right frequency so that we become aware of the messages that are being broadcast.

Still, I have often had doubts about the reality of the Committee. They say that doubt is part of the human condition. I recently experienced a big dose of that doubt. I was editing the sections on love, and my rational mind said: This is just too much! How can I possibly believe such good news in the face of what's happening in the world? For a day or two, I struggled with accepting the belief that Love is the animating force of the Universe, and that each of us is held in this Love. In spite of my ambivalence, I kept on working and noticed that the doubts gradually faded away. I share this to let you know that what the Committee says often stretches *my* perception of reality.

Here are some of the reasons why I trust what they teach:

• What they tell me is almost never what I am expecting to hear.

• Often when I ask a specific question, they use it as a springboard for speaking about something on *their* agenda.

• They continually surprise me. The content is usually about nothing that is in my conscious mind. Many times, the topic is one I'd prefer to avoid.

• Their language is very different from mine; it's often circuitous, repetitious, and poetic in a way that's not at all like my writing style.

• They are lighthearted. They take themselves much less seriously than I; they're playful in a way I'm not. They like to pun.

• Most importantly, I feel their ongoing love and presence in my day to day life. Occasionally, I sense their presence over my shoulder. It's subtle; they don't invade my privacy.

To make the Committee's words and ideas more accessible, I have arranged them into topics, but this is not the way I usually receive them. They might begin by saying, "We would speak of love," but soon they're talking about several other themes, often a new topic in each paragraph. They range and ramble, but in a wonderful way.

After writing down what they say and putting it aside, I can't remember the specifics. I have to read each transmission over and over to even begin to get the gist of what they're teaching me. Recently, a friend called to read a passage she thought might be instructive for me to hear again. The words were only vaguely familiar, but the message was powerful and hit me hard.

Often, I open the manuscript at random, or consult the table of contents to find the topic I need to read again. Their principles are few and simple but not easy, as they say. They assert that reality is Love; that we are cherished beings of creation, here in bodies to remember who we are and what we know. The Committee teaches that our assignment is to make love believable in the world through *us*.

I include some of the Committee's repetitions of their favorite themes. I know that *I* need to hear again and again the lessons about living with an open heart, letting go of struggle, and the notion of life as a journey back to Love.

Because the Committee's style is informal and conversational, I occasionally italicize words that they emphasize. I try to limit exclamation points. I capitalize their many words for God: the Source, the Universe, the One or Oneness, the Beloved, Divinity, Divine Mind, Creator, All That Is, the Giver, the Presence, the Essence of Being, Spirit, Love, Light. When Spirit is used as a name for God, I capitalize it; when spirit describes the soul, I use the lower case. When the Committee uses love, light and divinity as synonyms for God or Spirit, I capitalize them. When they are used as qualities I don't. But sometimes the distinction between deity and quality isn't entirely clear, in which cases I do my best to sort out the meaning. When they use the metaphor of 'the Path' as our life journey, I capitalize Path.

A few additional details: I try to alternate using gender-specific pronouns. The questions in the text are occasionally from me, but most often from others.

Introduction

Regarding reincarnation, the Committee never addresses this directly, but it's clear from their many references to it, that they treat it as a given. I denote separate transmissions with the symbol ∽ⓔ∽.

Occasionally, I include parts of my personal story that point to my search for meaning, and my connection to the Committee. These sections are in *italics*.

A word about the contemporary channeling phenomenon: ever since I read *The Search for Bridey Murphy* many years ago, I have been intrigued by the world of spirit and the possibility of reincarnation. I have been moved by the writings of contemporary channels. I've also wondered whether some who claimed to be channeling wrote or spoke from ego rather than inspiration. Most of all, I dislike the word 'channel' because it's often made fun of and mocked in the media. Then I found that I could be described that way myself. It seemed like a joke that life was playing on me.

Finally, I have stopped trying to figure out how my otherwise normal life story fits with this experience of channeling the Committee. My connection to them seems to be an anomaly in my life—one I'm incredibly grateful for, but an anomaly all the same.

I'm aware of the great privilege I have to share the Committee's teachings with you. I feel strongly that these writings are not just for me, but for everyone whose hearts are open to understand and experience reality in these new and hopeful ways. The longer I live with the Committee, the more I'm convinced that their teachings are exactly what I need for *my* human and spiritual development. I hope, as you read their words, they will have meaning for you as well.

The Committee's Story

Most of us have been part of your world, some of us many times. We remember life in a body and have great compassion for its challenges. Our names, and where and when we lived, are mere details and not of our essence. We remember our pasts with nostalgia, but the purpose of our communication with you is not reminiscence. At our collaborator's suggestion, we sign off as The Committee. We like this title because it's impersonal; it reflects our comings and goings according to the tasks we've chosen. This is how a committee works, isn't it? A committee is constant, with the membership changing as necessary.

We are now in a clearer *state* of being, which is different from a physical *place* of being. Light and Love surround us. We are not dependent on the senses for information. You won't fully understand this until you're here. Of course you have *been* here, but you agree to forget when you take on a body.

We are still discovering truth, but in spirit it's easier to learn. It is our pleasure and our assignment to share what we are learning. This is a time when the boundaries between our realities are becoming more permeable. We are here to help you remember what you already know and have forgotten. Forgetting is part of the illusion, the game of agreeing to be a human being. *And* it's a game you can learn to play successfully and lightheartedly.

We offer you our thoughts from a place where ego is no longer an issue, where lessons are learned in joy, and struggle and fear are seen as illusion. Since we are not bound by fear any longer, we are able to walk in the Light every moment, and share with you what we've learned, and continue to learn, on our journeys.

Our connection with you is a choice of love for us. This is a special moment in human evolution—a time of revelation. We are able to bridge the worlds of form and formlessness; to be a link between material and spiritual dimensions. Bridges are necessary at first, particularly if you're making your way cautiously from one side to the other. We are delighted to be your bridges at this stage in your spiritual development. But remember, bridges are unnecessary if you fly!

Our mutual boundaries are weakening so there can be more conscious collaboration between humans and those of us who are in spirit. In these times, the same truths are being proclaimed in many places, but there is never competition where truth is told. Those who are open to these truths will be led to them. There are no accidents. Your steps are lovingly guided.

~⚬~

That summer evening in Vermont was the beginning of our transmissions on the physical plane with Maureen as our collaborator. How does this process of communication work? On a soul level, Maureen agrees to let us use her time, mind and vocabulary. Her consciousness moves over slightly, and allows us to transmit our thoughts through the vehicle of her mind. She writes, types or speaks as we dictate. Sometimes she helps find the best word or phrase as we translate down into human language. Her discipline is to write without thinking or worrying about what comes next. This exercise of putting one word in front of another becomes a kind of meditation.

We are separate from her *and* a part of her. She feels both dimensions, not as a dichotomy, but more as a blending. Her intelligence is an appropriate vehicle through which we're able to work, and she has agreed to be used to transmit these ideas. It's an integrated, elegant collaboration; one that is very common among you, but most often unconscious. What makes this communication with Maureen unusual is that she *knows* what's happening. There is also an element of *not knowing* in her, which is equally important in keeping her personality out of the process as much as possible. She needs to be focused, detached, and not in the least invested in the outcome.

She is a clear channel, even when she doesn't think she is. Our collaboration doesn't depend on her feelings. For her, it's a matter of being willing, temporarily, to set aside her ego, judgment and fear. Although her task is to keep ego out of the process, this doesn't mean that she's not ultimately in charge. We always seek her permission as a colleague.

We trust that our words are a confirmation of what many of you already know: that there is in this era a close connection between those in the physical world on the Path of conscious intention and their non-physical friends who share this Path.

1

A New Model of Reality

Only Love is Real.

Y ou are a spiritual child of the Universe. You have
a right not only to be here, but to be happy and
fulfilled through meaningful work and play. You
have not been dumped onto the earth by a biological accident. All coming to life is a choice. It's a choice to be
claimed again and again, so that you *remember* you have
chosen to be in a body.

The Source of the cosmos, called by many names—God,

A New Model of Reality

Yahweh, Jesus, Allah—knows you by name, has named you for eternity. The name you now bear is transitory. Spirit has named your eternal essence. When you remember that you are a named being of the Universe, you walk the Path. *You* open the channel and Spirit has access to *you*.

You are here in this physical reality now to practice *being*. You don't need to learn how to be—you simply are, now and from forever to forever. The more you experience that you *are*, the more the doing that follows from being is informed by your conscious awareness of eternal safety. Being is the opposite of struggle and control; it empowers the mind to innovate and improvise. Then, doing becomes the way you realize your unique being in time. When doing takes its proper place, time appears to magically expand. It's no longer the slave driver that runs your life. But being isn't sitting around daydreaming, or expecting to be rescued by magic. We understand that the bills need to be paid and the floors vacuumed, but we speak of your purpose for coming into the world.

Being is the practice of getting in touch with your soul's priorities. Every soul has an agenda for each incarnation.

Some goals are common to everyone, while others are specific to *your* life path. Your unique plan cannot be discovered in the midst of the world's busyness. It is discovered in the silent space that your soul needs to share this plan with you.

ETERNAL SAFETY

Sink into the embrace of Spirit. Dare to fall backward, trusting there is no abyss. Life is not a problem to be solved. It is a willingness to be present to the energy that holds everyone and everything in existence. You can never be estranged from the All That Is, even for a millisecond. There is no possibility of falling through the cracks into a void. There *are* no cracks and there *is* no void. The cracks are an illusion, and you're here to push through illusion.

In the presence of worldly danger, long held beliefs proclaim that you aren't safe, you might die, your loved ones might suffer. Although such events happen in the context of the world's illusion, no one is in danger and no one ever dies, in the sense of ceasing to exist. Suffering, no matter how intense, cannot harm the soul of any human.

You can frighten yourself by dire imaginings, but your spirit's survival is never in jeopardy. From this perspective, you are able to view the circumstances of your life with less drama.

You are eternally safe because you are held in the love of the Creator. If you can't believe this, be with your doubts and don't judge where you are. When you begin to believe that you are safe and loved, a new vista opens up. Then you are able to release limiting beliefs that have endured throughout human history—that life ends in death, or that your soul will survive only to be judged by a wrathful God. The revolutionary truth is that you are exquisitely cared for and loved every moment of your existence. There is no way you can fall out of Love—this is what safety means.

We remind you that Love is no less real in the presence of cruelty and disaster. Life's challenges cannot destroy you, because you are held forever in a web of eternal Love. When you see past life's illusions, then life reveals itself as a game, or a course of study, but not one to be taken too seriously.

Even when everything seems to be falling apart you are

safe—not necessarily comfortable, but safe. It doesn't matter whether friends and lovers are true or untrue, whether children are easy or challenging, whether you're rich or poor, healthy or sick—your safety is guaranteed. When you are aware of living life in the context of eternal safety, you become audacious. You dare to take risks and challenge commonly held beliefs.

Calling danger's bluff opens up to you a new world of possibility and abundance, where expectation becomes a powerful tool for fashioning your life. Danger is not your adversary; it's often simply the way you label the unknown. Fortunately, the more you let go of fear, the more elegantly and easily the unknown becomes known. It's not a matter of giving up, but of gently releasing the desire for control.

Humans have believed so profoundly, and for so long, in the reality of danger that it creates its own reality. When you believe in danger, you live within its illusion. As you experience danger and *choose* to see it as illusion, you remember that you are safe in the embrace of Spirit. This is reality—not sentimental claptrap or opiate for the masses.

Because your eternal safety is assured, this doesn't mean

that nothing is required of you in the world. But worry is the one thing that is *not* required. Worrying about the details of the future inhibits your intuition and creativity. As you let go of worry, even when there seem to be valid reasons for anxiety, you discover that you won't perish. Instead, you begin to experience that you live in the heart of Love and can never be moved from this place, except by the illusion of your own forgetting.

THE PATH OF CONSCIOUS AWARENESS

The world of Spirit reveals itself as you take the time to be silent, to meditate and to read the articles and books that attract you. You begin to be nudged by synchronicity; you have serendipitous encounters with others who are fellow seekers. It's not that this new reality was previously inaccessible, but now you recognize the signs.

Train yourself to become aware of the promptings of Spirit. You'll acquire the confidence to listen and act on what you're learning. Be fully present to every moment, to each sound, word, color, breath. Full openness to the present moment is all that is ever asked of you—not even asked; it's more like an invitation to participate fully in consciousness.

This new sense of awareness of your soul expands your feelings of worth as you recognize that you're making changes that affect the quality of your life. You'll notice a surge in your creativity and energy. Although you're in charge of when to embark on this journey, you are never alone. You begin to be aware that spiritual helpers are present, and as you ask for their help, they become more available to you.

Becoming conscious is about waking up from the dream. It's about letting go of illusions and fantasies. It's about stripping away all that isn't essential to take with you on your journey. Waking up means you're showing up for life, saying, "Here I am, reporting for duty."

What is the journey about and where is it taking you? When you are on the path of conscious awareness, you agree to go inward to the core of your being and to examine what you find there. You trust life and its purposes. You let go of expectations. This new model of reality is designed to be put into practice. Then it becomes more than hypothesis; it is *experienced* as reality.

A New Model of Reality

TRANSFORMING DUALITY

The world you know is pre-eminently a place of duality. But when you acknowledge duality and accept it for what it is, it transforms into something quite different. When you view the earth experience as a game, the magician's trick is exposed as a clever sleight of hand. As you recognize duality, you are able to go beyond it. You taste joy in a way that would be impossible if you'd never known sadness. If you never experienced anything but unalloyed delight, you might fail to appreciate it. You experience the antithesis of joy so that you *know* the difference.

Our words are always variations on the theme that Love is the only reality. Love is present in places of human degradation, in selfishness and violence. Negative human experiences take place in the context of Love. Love's opposites are part of the vast panoply of lessons that humans choose.

Sickness, sadness and lack are temporary. Tears and grief are reminders that you are more than bodies, intellects and emotions. You are also part of Love. Only Love is real and eternal. All the attempts to create theologies are efforts to express this one encompassing reality.

You participate out of necessity in this Love force. You are part of the limitless energy that is you and every created being, star and universe—all expressions of Love made visible. From this perspective, all life experience can be seen in the context of Love revealing itself in humans as they evolve to higher consciousness. Even when the challenges of the earth plane veil the reality of Love, it is no less real. In spite of ignorance, greed and cruelty, earth is moving toward the realization of Love in all things.

RETRAINING THE MIND

In this new model of reality, the mind is revealed as a magnificent tool *and* a demanding companion. It creates solutions from its knowledge, experience and intuition. Because you are held in the context of a more inclusive, wiser intelligence than mind's knowing, you know much more than is necessary to solve a problem. Your head can become paralyzed, however, when useful information mixes with fear. When you allow Spirit as the coordinator of your mind, feelings and body, the mind is free to be creative and function optimally in a new expanded way.

You can *change* your mind; you can retrain its habitual negative thoughts. The conversion from negative to positive begins and is sustained by the power of your intention. Learning a new habit of mind is challenging, and, of course, you can't internalize a new way of being if it becomes yet another heavy burden. The new consciousness that is emerging is literally of the Light, and can be achieved more efficiently with a light heart.

As you begin to retrain your mind, you become aware of its habit of tuning in to the static of random chatter. The more you accept your mind with its natural inclinations, the calmer it can become. When old patterns arise, stop in mid-thought. Forgive your brain's wanderings and return your attention to the breath—this is the easiest way of refocusing. The focused mind can more easily get out of the way when you ask for access to higher intelligence. This is the opposite of losing your mind; it's expanding it to connect with Universal Mind.

Your spirit has outlived many of your minds. The

Source of intelligence, of which you are a part, transcends the particular finite mind connected to your body. A mind, no matter how bright, can accomplish relatively little. But when connected with deeper wisdom, your native intelligence becomes a collaborator with higher mind.

Reality is not some fixed set of circumstances into which you must squeeze yourself. It is your child, your creation, your love for yourself made visible. Your mind's thoughts are real; they have power. This power is neutral and can work positively or negatively.

Possibility begins with desire. Not a wishy-washy desire that says—I'd *like* this to be, but it's probably not possible. Such a thought impedes the realization of your longing. Instead, hold the desire in your mind, trusting that it is in the process of becoming manifest. What needs changing is not so much the present reality, but your way of *thinking* about it. It is possible to re-program your habitual thoughts, but first you must become aware of your negative thought patterns.

When you notice yourself thinking a disempowering

thought, you need to gently but firmly send that thought on its way. It's important at this point not to judge the thought or yourself for having the thought. Judgment is self-defeating. *Attention* is the way to change old habits of mind. When these new habits are well established, such meticulous attention is less necessary.

Your deepest needs are always being met—even when experience seems to provide strong evidence to the contrary. When an old lesson, one you're tired of, shows up in your life again, it presents itself so that you become so fed up with it, that *this* time may be the last. And the mind asks— do I really have control over circumstances that sap my energy and encroach on my time? The power to control and change events in your outer reality starts with an inner change of mind.

On a spiritual level, all created beings, whether in a body or not, share the same needs, desires and goals. Our common need is to strip away all that isn't essential for the journey. This means guarding our thoughts and choosing what we pay attention to. This heightened awareness requires attention and discipline.

This model of how to live in the world requires tending, like a new garden. Before plantings become established in the ground they require care, but after a while it becomes easier. The plants are on their way, with only occasional support from the gardener. It's the same with the seedlings of positive thoughts. Old habits are well established, so these loving, non-judgmental seedlings will at first require careful weeding. Don't be discouraged—discouragement is just another weed. The process gets easier, even fun.

LIVING IN THE MOMENT

Heaven is not a home in the sky. Heaven is here, now, living in the present moment. Hell is not a fire that burns to punish you for your sins. Hell is not being in the now. *Hell is later, then, when, if, if only.*

Be in the moment as the fabric of your life swirls around you—the pen on the paper, the crow cawing in the distance, the air cooling your skin, the clouds skimming across the sky, the dappled sunlight and shade on the grass. This moment, then the next, and the next. *Experience* each one instead of steeling yourself against anticipated pain. *Be* the pain when it comes; let it wash over you. There is nothing to fear in this process. Instead, what you discover is a profound and sweet freedom from fear.

The way to accomplish great things is by doing small things well and consciously in each moment. This focus in the present is the opposite of stressful striving. It is a decision to live in the now. Being in the moment is all that's ever required of you, but it's the most challenging discipline. We don't suggest that you neglect to make sensible plans or do necessary tasks. But the discipline of *now* means giving up worry about the next moment or the next day, because now is all there is. When you step into the Oneness of which you are a part, you go beyond linear time to a place of pure being, pure now. Then you are fully present to every moment.

Do what you're doing fully until it's time to stop. Then do what's next in the same mindful way. When you're washing the car, *really* wash it, instead of rushing through the job as you rehearse in your head what you're going to do next. Life becomes simple when reduced to its moments. It's impossible to be where you're not supposed to be. Everything that happens is for your learning. Your tutorial is uniquely yours and may seem glacially slow, but the lessons are all happening in their perfect time.

Your energy and focus will increase as a result of your self-love, while self-judgment depletes you. Gently send on their way judgment, regret, guilt, and pushing against your body's needs. You fully honor your place in creation by doing the work of each moment. This way of being awake requires vigilance. Slipping back into stress and self-judgment is what many of you have been conditioned to do, but you no longer have to live your days in this knee-jerk negative way. You have a choice about how to respond in each moment and circumstance, and you have the privilege of practicing this new way of living.

Practice being—not striving or worrying, not even hoping or planning. We know this is difficult in its simplicity. It's hard to think about being; you simply *are*. But the *awareness* of being creates an open space for Spirit to work. Then there's no need to push, because you're in the flow of life.

Doing, without an awareness of the moment, diminishes the quality of your life. In the middle of whirlwind activity, deadlines to meet, miles to travel, practice becoming centered, unmoved and unmovable in your being. You play the game of life more successfully when you know what is real and what is illusion. When a day is seen in this light, the bits fall into their rightful places. Then, nothing is out of place. Every happening is perfect, even in its apparent imperfection. From an eternal perspective, time passes according to the plan of your higher self.

Don't expect the worst—better yet, don't even expect. Let life surprise you! Every moment has its own sweetness. It presents an opportunity for you to choose each thought, each act, from a loving place. You have everything you need for this moment and the next. You can decide to stand in the sunshine, to trust the unknown as you walk toward it.

Your experience in the world, however, teaches you that plans often go awry. But there is planning that comes from ego and planning that comes from Spirit. *This* kind of planning is open-ended, open-hearted. *This* planning is open to a change of route, to unexpected outcomes, to serendipitous happenings. It's a level of planning that integrates head and heart, mind and spirit. Then the ego's desires are held in the context of Love's knowing. This kind of planning allows you to live in the moment while at the same time preparing for a possible future. This is living response-ably.

When you're open to all experience with child-like trust, you may become aware of an acceleration of delightful change in your life. New energies in the form of persons and ways of attracting abundance become available to you. These changes are a confirmation that you are working cooperatively with Spirit.

Work with available energy, not against it. Make the best possible decision you can in each moment. Sometimes the task is to do something; sometimes it's to back off and set limits. When you follow your energy, you learn when to push past resistance and when to yield to it. Find balance, respect your limits, and do forgive yourself when you make mistakes.

The path to today has been protected through all your wanderings, your lost and found ways. All were a route to today. Some yesterdays were full, some empty and lost, burdened by grief. Each of the days was the perfect day for that day. We remind you so that you remember to trust the days not yet here.

Living in the now is so simple it seems difficult; it's so simple that most humans don't believe they can do it. Many avoid it because they believe their whole lives have to change in order to come into the present moment. Life *will* change, but it's a subtle inner shift. When you practice living this way, you begin to notice a new clarity. When this shift is made again and again, outer changes may happen quickly and dramatically.

You may experience the stream of events in the now on a surface level, reacting to each in a kind of automatic way—annoyed, angry, pleased, relieved. Or, you can notice these reactive tendencies and at the same time choose to experience the event or circumstance from the eternal present. Holy ones, whom you call saints, practice viewing events in the light of eternity, but this is not an exercise reserved only for the ascetic. You can use it to make your own life run more smoothly.

When life is unfathomable in its apparent lack of meaning, then you have a special opportunity to practice living in the moment. Sit in the awareness of your heart space and be still enough to learn its wisdom. This is the opposite of anxious activity. It is a cessation of activity, of strategy, even of thinking. When you are present to the moment, you come into the presence of your soul.

LIVING WITH AN OPEN HEART

In the midst of whatever is happening, we invite you to keep your heart open. The lesson of lessons, the one that informs all the others, is to become conscious of living from your heart. Instead of denying your feelings, keep your heart open as the feelings wash over you. Notice all the missteps into judgment and fear, and make the adjustments back to a loving place. In this way, the negative emotions can move on. What remains is the love that sustains all things.

A New Model of Reality

Remember, you are on the Path *you* have chosen. You are where and with whom you are supposed to be at every moment. We remind you to be patient with your personality on this self-selected Path. You have come here to do your soul work within the limitations of time and a body. This poses challenges, but not impossible ones.

Experience is what life is offering you in this moment and the next. Your heart's longing is revealed in the present moment, yet the seduction of illusion is strong. In this moment, you may be distracted from your longing by worry, wealth, poverty, or lack of trust in the process of living from the heart. You can accept all of life with an open heart, or you can make the judgment that life is unfair. All the disparate experiences of your life are under the protection of Spirit. Being on the Path doesn't mean that you're excused from experiences—both the pleasurable ones that feel like blessings, and the difficult ones that seem like burdens. It's what you do with your experience and how you use it that makes all the difference. Instead of closing your heart and running from pain, use these opportunities to open your heart and discover the lessons there.

Visualize light filling your heart center and emanating to all parts of you. This is not to be taken on as a kind of dutiful discipline. Tension and grim determination close the heart. It opens only as you relax. Then, love goes where it goes, and you're more able to receive as well as give.

You'll know you've got the knack of opening your heart when you become aware that doing it is a pleasure, then a necessity—something you can't live without, as necessary as breath filling your lungs. Not unconscious breathing that keeps the body alive; rather, conscious breathing that chooses to be in the presence of Love.

The discipline is to be aware of your heart center, to have the intention to be open to love, to do no harm, consciously or unconsciously. This practice of returning to your open heart will keep you focused on your purpose here. You will fulfill this purpose because it is an agreement you have made with your spirit.

The goal is to strip away all that is not love: to let go of everything that distracts you from being in the presence of Love and from being an expression of that Love. Then the details of your life won't matter as much to you. You will begin to release the struggle for your preferences. It's not that you give up your preferences; instead, you practice holding them in your open heart. Then, whatever happens becomes your preference. You choose *all* of life, regardless of how the outer circumstances may appear. Life becomes sweet in its simplicity when you begin to live this way.

Now is a time in earth's history when everyone who wakes up is crucial to the evolution, even the survival, of the human species. Humans have the technology now to annihilate humankind. This potential for destruction is the wake-up call beyond all wake-up calls. It is also a moment pregnant with potential for an evolved consciousness to be shared by all humans. This unparalleled opportunity will begin for you when you make the choice, in every interaction, to live with an open heart.

2

From Struggle to Joy

*When you do what you love,
work is synonymous with play.*

hen you begin to struggle, water can no longer hold you up. Discover that it's safe to lie back and float. The grand illusion of the earth plane is that you must struggle against sorrows and tragedy that threaten to engulf you. It's difficult to ignore this illusion because humans have believed so long in struggle as a way of life.

Struggle appears so that you can learn how to release it. Struggle is always a choice. But letting go of it can become a *conscious* choice. The paradox is to acknowledge the struggle and simultaneously release it. Do what you can, what is practical and possible, then let go of the outcome.

The choice to lay down the burden of struggle is not an act of irresponsibility, but one of response-ability. In order to be best able to respond appropriately, it's helpful to carry as little baggage as possible. This will free your creative responses for the challenges and opportunities that life offers. Try *not* working hard. Have the intention to be in the stream of effortless creativity. This is how all great creative breakthroughs are accomplished.

As you go about your tasks, remember the importance of self-love. Every time you are tempted to rush, to berate yourself, to push in a tense habitual way—stop, and be fully in the task of the moment. This is a way to transform the task into one of satisfaction and fulfillment.

What if you were to claim and use your gifts? The result would be an elegant simplicity. All that is not of your Path would fall away effortlessly. Struggle is an expression of duality. When you make choices in the awareness of your highest purpose you become integrated with that purpose. Then you learn lessons without struggle, so that they don't need to be repeated. Your time is free to spend in the development of your own deepest knowing.

When you make the decision to let go of struggle, creativity flourishes and serendipitous events happen because you're in the flow, not paddling madly against the current. It's so simple to live this way that it may seem impossible until you try. But when you make this choice, there's no sense of 'trying' about it. You live in the present moment, one breath at a time.

The Path is never one of struggle. Struggle is always a sign that you are off course. It's a sure sign of trying to figure things out in the old way—of trying to whip the mind into submission. You can choose to end struggle and gain the freedom, time and means to be your most creative self. Make this new choice often, since the mind needs to learn new patterns. But don't do it with clenched teeth; view the retraining as a healthy support for your life, not as a battle.

When old patterns come up, stop in mid-thought, and remember what you know. The mind is just the portal, the gate of knowledge. Wisdom is of the heart, purely intuitive, unencumbered by linear thinking. It knows in a way the mind is not designed to know. This is a time in the evolution of many for old mind habits to emerge from their long dormancy into conscious awareness. Once you look at these habits as choice, your life can never again be lived in the same automatic way. Change has begun, however imperceptibly.

Crises are opportunities for trusting your own wisdom. As you notice yourself struggling, you have an opportunity to love yourself by stepping back and looking around. During a crisis, love yourself first, then extend that love out to others and ask to be in the stream of creativity. This will allow you to find solutions more easily. Think of these new ways of dealing with problems as an experiment to be tried with a light heart and a sense of curiosity. The old ways clearly don't work.

When you need to do things that don't speak to your heart, do them lightly. Then they occupy little psychic space, and don't deplete your energy. The more you open your heart, the more these peripheral things can fall away. Living with ease happens naturally when you focus on your ever-present connection to the Light. This Light within you is a resource waiting to be tapped, especially in the darkest times.

Can you be fully in the world with its demands and yet be simultaneously at a deeper place of peace and centeredness? Can you touch this dual reality without retreating to a monastic cell? Can you be happy in your body and yet know that this physical disguise is not to be taken too seriously? The answer is yes. If the 'demands' of your life are handled with the part of you that is efficient and lighthearted, they become reduced to doable tasks. You can be busy without becoming anxious.

PAIN AS OPPORTUNITY

In the dark night of the soul, when you slide and fall on the chaotic surface of events, and there seems no direction, no comfort, no connection to Spirit, dare to be the confusion and the not-knowing. Surrender to it. You may discover that your deepest pain is your friend and teacher.

Painful events are steps along the Path, and you get sidetracked only if you stop and obsess about them. You've asked for these events on some level; they're part of an ongoing purification and preparation process. Use what life offers you. Even the most awful and apparently meaningless disaster can be used in some way toward your transformation.

You have chosen to live on this plane of polarity where events happen that make no sense to your mind. Although painful, these events are actually happening on the periphery of your life, this life that is protected through every experience. We don't presume to minimize difficulties. Losses are real. Have you been singled out for loss? We say unequivocally, no. Can you use loss to deepen your journey here? Absolutely. The key is to have the audacity to keep your heart open in the midst of any event that threatens to seduce you into becoming disheartened.

Difficulties are opportunities to clear out old habits. They can accomplish their purpose best if they're not feared, simply acknowledged, dealt with and moved through as efficiently as possible. Don't shrink from a time of testing and growth. Dare to flow with it. If you reject challenges out of fear, they'll appear again, because Spirit offers the lesson over and over until there's no longer any need for it. The simile of life as a schoolroom is a good one—just lessons to be learned, stages of growth on the Path.

All human drama is part of the passing show. Pain is just pain, the polarity of joy. Hold it lightly and let it heal you. This gentle being with pain makes room for joy. And let joy take you by surprise. Joy is always present, no less so because you're unaware of it.

There may be times when your life is chaotic. You may experience loss on many levels—financial ruin, physical illness, the death of a beloved. So the question returns—how can you live successfully, fully in this place of darkness and light, tragedy and joy, rationality and incomprehensibility? We challenge you to trust your life and everyone's life here. Earth is sometimes a place of intense, uncomfortable learning—yet it is also a place of great joy.

You are held in a cocoon of protection no matter what

happens. Those who persist in killing one another are in no danger as they lie bloody in the streets. All who died on September 11 have moved on to new adventures. The challenge is greatest for the ones left behind to deal with loss and find meaning in it.

I'm very discouraged about my daughter's relapse into alcoholism. How can I cope with this?

Her pain is her pain. When she has had enough, she'll stop creating it. Allow her to be in her pain, and be unattached to any outcome. She's in no danger, even if she were to lose her life. She is on the Path as surely as the most enlightened being, even if the route looks circuitous and burdensome. She is safe, perfectly safe, as she flails away. Keep your heart open, send her love, and hold her in the Light as you allow her to be in her struggle. She has chosen this struggle on her Path. The task of a parent is to step back in love. So much of loving is letting go, particularly with your children. But your children are never lost to you. The connection remains throughout eternity.

Out of the blue, my wife announced she's leaving me. What's the purpose of this pain in my life? How can I make meaning out of this heartache?

The events of your life that press down on you so intensely are opportunities to learn, or more precisely, to remember what you already know. In the place where your undiminished being is eternally present, you know who you are beyond your personality.

You may ask—what solace is this for my heart when my life is in chaos? How can I trust that all is well? Trust comes in the doing, in the stepping out. Trusting life's larger purpose affirms your willingness to be on the Path without knowing the destination. We know how this goes against the grain, how your mind resists *being* rather than knowing. But it's impossible to know in the way your mind wants to know. You've chosen your personality through which to express yourself. Although the way isn't easy, you do have control over its difficulty; it can be as rocky or as smooth as you decide it will be.

When you choose clearly, circumstances have less power over you. It's not that this choice, once made, excuses you from all responsibility for your actions. It's that the choice informs your decisions, your actions, and most importantly, your attitudes. Then upsetting circumstances become opportunities for soul growth. They can be struggled against or they can be sailed through. You can choose to ride the waves of circumstance that you can't control. You can sail with the wind at your back or you can hide in the hold of the ship, not daring to enjoy the passing seascape. Events don't have the power to hurt you unless you give them permission.

Keep your heart open during a time of many unknowns, and ask for the protection of the highest energy. You have come with all the resources you need for this trip. You are enough for you.

Work as Play

Trust the Universe and what it offers you. Accept it all with curiosity and a sense of playfulness. You are much too serious most of the time. Doing your true work in the world was never meant to be a somber affair. It's the ultimate paradox to be in the flow when you're in the midst of struggle.

Work doesn't have to be something you tolerate to make money to support yourself or your family. When work is aligned with your purpose, the artificial boundaries between work and play begin to dissolve. Authentic work doesn't feel like work; it's more like effortless pleasure. Work is labor only if it doesn't bring you joy. When you do what you love, work is synonymous with play. And when work is play, the process flows. If you're weary of the belief that life is hard work, try a little experiment. Give up trying hard. It's part of the new model of reality. Act as if life were high play. All you have to lose is exhaustion and stress. This new way of living is so simple that it seems impossible. We point only to the unworkability and heartache of the old way.

Humans have invented hard work and struggle. Ease and joy are of the Creator. Do you think for a moment that Love struggled or worked hard to manifest the magnificent cosmos? The Universe flows from Spirit's love, as a child comes from human love.

Do what you love and what you do well. In this way,

you create the time for realizing your deepest needs. Your work is you—literally! It is you manifesting in the world, peeling away layers of 'not you' in order to come to what is uniquely you. Your challenge is to let go of whatever prevents *you* from happening.

When you follow your joy and your energy, love is truly your work. Joseph Campbell said to "follow your bliss." There comes a time to catch up with it, to enter into the bliss and become one with it. Then everything is done and seen from this luminous perspective. The Path becomes smooth and the focus clear.

I am waiting tables to support myself when I want to be writing, doing what I love and what will make the biggest contribution. By the time I get home, I'm too tired to write.

Keep releasing ideas of hard work, hurry, and stress. When these notions pester you, gently send them away again and again. There is nothing to do, ever, than to be in the present moment. Take the order, serve the meal, clear the table. In this way, your life reveals itself to you. You become a partner in its unfolding plan, not a drill sergeant whipping the troops of your personality into line. This unfolding of the greater plan cannot happen in the midst of push and shove. It happens when you take a step back and observe your life without judgment.

Some ways of spending time are more in tune with your soul's purpose than others, but no matter what you're doing, it's not possible to be off the Path. Let your inner work guide your outer work, no matter how mundane it may seem. Be patient and love yourself through times of transition, when it seems that the Universe is not responding to your requests. It's important to be willing to do what is necessary for human survival. As you look back one day, you'll be able to make sense out of what seemed to make no sense.

Hold your highest intention no matter how the world seems to be responding. When you have the intention to be aligned with your highest energy, your purpose is protected. Maintain an inner confidence and calm in circumstances that might have caused you anxiety in the past. The ways of Love are often mysterious and confounding to the mind.

As more of you stand your ground in this way, new ways

of working and living in the world become possible. Your collective intention and action will initiate these changes. There will be miracles of change, and you will be the change agents. Holding lightly the work of the old paradigm allows it to fall away.

Your purpose here cannot go unfulfilled unless you say a conscious no. Your assignment for now is to show up to wait those tables, listen for guidance, still the chattering mind, and be patient with the process. There is never anything to fear in the working out of your purpose here. The phrase 'working out' is an inherent flaw in your language. Your reason for coming can be fulfilled so much more easily if you 'play it out.' A light heart is the way. Tension and exhaustion are beliefs to be gently released. Accept the revolutionary idea that life is play.

LIVING IN JOY

Joy is the quality that opens your mind to the next level of learning. Joy is the catalyst for the 'Aha!', the creative insight born of new relationships you discover among previously unconnected ideas. Joy is the medium in which great creative advances happen. Huge amounts of energy may be required to compose the music, publish the research or conduct the experiments, but the conception happens in joy.

Being open to creativity doesn't always result in a product. It is a way of being. Living in joy ends forever your old life of anxious striving. It breaks open the heart. You stand in a vulnerability to life that is both exquisitely protected and in the flow of the creative force of the Universe. From this place, desires become manifest. So step out onto the Path with no bags packed and no set itinerary. Be willing to trust life's goodness and your own high purpose. For a life of joy—embrace the Universe and its manifestations, and love yourself by choosing, in each decision, what makes you happy.

You are in charge of the joy in your life. Doing what you love is your job in this lifetime. Forcing yourself to do what you hate is intrinsically self-defeating. Do nothing, ever, out of a sense of should. What a terrible way to treat such a loving being! Your life is not a puzzle to be solved. When joy dissolves the illusion of life as a puzzle, it appears before you, whole and clear.

Imagine what could happen to the economy, to military spending, to every aspect of your lives, if joy were the bottom line! You *can* choose to live in joy. It is an act of will—not a strategy or a struggle. The choice is not between struggle and giving up; the choice is between struggle and joy. From our perspective, it is hard to imagine not choosing joy. If you view patterns of struggle and pain as choices, your life can never again be lived in the same way.

Change from struggle to joy can simmer slowly for many years or many lifetimes. During these times, not much will change in the outer world. But inner and outer change can also happen quickly, almost simultaneously. The catalyst for change is refusing to believe the bad news.

What if you experimented with the possibility that joy is your natural state? Would this change your outer reality? Would it transform your frail, fearful grandmother into a woman of poise and grace? Would it change your suspicious landlord into a being of light? (Of course, he *is* a being of light!) Would it make your angry, rebellious teenager relaxed and trusting? Maybe, maybe not. But when you give up the need to change others' behavior, you shift your perception of them; you let go of *your* struggle and suspicion.

You need your own permission to be happy. Happiness is not a reward for good deeds. It is a stance, a choice to live your life in joy.

Joy is the reality that is so overlooked in the world's emphasis on catastrophe, corrupt politics, poverty, worry. We remind you that joy is the primary building block of creation. Joy is present in the chaos of a natural disaster. Joy is present in the rough and tumble of politics. Joy is present in incurable cancer. It is present as a soul prepares to slough off the body.

Notice the joy in music, in art, in elegant writing, in a delicious meal, in the snow falling, softening the starkness of the winter landscape. Notice the joy in a baby's delight in living fully in the present. Most importantly, find the joy in you. If there is a place in your old conditioning that believes in a wrathful God, gently release that belief. Spirit is Love—simple as that. The way to this joy is to embrace the tasks and sensations of each moment, its pleasures and challenges. Notice feelings and reactions as they pass by—not judging, simply noticing. Pay attention to gratitude. Embrace a simple, elegant theology that assumes love is at the core of every thing and experience.

3

Healing Your Fear

Fear works, love plays.
Fear inhibits, love frees.
Fear hesitates, love leaps into the unknown.
Love trusts itself.

It was Sunday, the day before my father's funeral. We had all gone to Mass, and I prayed something like, "Okay God, I surrender. Whatever you want for me is okay."

That evening, I was sprawled on the bed in my parents' guest room, trying to get the protocol right for an Irish

Catholic funeral. This is how it works: the people less close to the deceased—co-workers, second cousins, friends, leave the funeral home first and get into the farthest cars in the procession. On and on until the immediate family is the last to leave the room where the body is displayed, and where they say their last goodbyes.

If you make a mistake, certain relatives are sure to be offended. So there I was, struggling with this task, when suddenly, I was suffused with a love I couldn't imagine existed. It was visceral. It came in through my head and filled me with the most sublime peace. I began to cry, not from grief, but from the intensity of the love. At some point, I began to feel afraid. The magnitude of it all seemed more than I could handle. As fear crept in, the experience began to fade.

Yet, the effect of such palpable love was that I was able to go through my dad's funeral in a state of joy. I couldn't understand why people were praying for 'the repose of his soul.' I knew that my father was safe, and learning to make his way in the dimension of spirit.

Y ou don't have to wait for some disembodied future to overcome fear. You can learn while in a body, within the limitations of time, space and matter. Each time you remember to let go of fear, you'll notice there is less and less of it. But don't deny your feelings. Repressing them is what prevents feelings from moving on.

There are as many variations on fear as there are human beings. There is fear of success as well as failure, fear of doing and of not doing, fear of making mistakes, fear, ultimately, of *not* being.

Your eternal life cannot *not* be; it simply *is*. In one sense it is linear; in another, it is all-present in each moment. You are *of* life, *in* life, of its very essence. Without you, life could not be as it is. You are essential to life, your spirit both a discrete and an indivisible part of the whole. When you trust this safety from annihilation, you are able to fully experience your aliveness.

The fear that lives with you is your teacher. It is a reminder of the process of growth going on in your soul. As you become more conscious, hidden fears are revealed. The fears you discover don't need your judgment. Hold them in the light of Love and gently ask them what they need from you.

It helps to go inside and have a little heart-to-heart with the fear you find there. It's not with you as a cruel taskmaster. Fear signals the possibility of a breakthrough for your spirit. It points to what your soul is ready to work on next. This doesn't mean that you must work through each issue of fear that comes up, but the fear always surfaces because at some deep level, you're ready to deal with it.

A time when fear arises is a potentially powerful moment. Feel your fear, be with it and in it, then practice moving the fear through you. The problem is not that fear comes, but that it gets stuck. If you dismiss or deny it, it will become like plaque in the arteries, clogging up the works.

The tricky part is experiencing the feelings fear engenders. You may believe that fear will overwhelm you and catapult you into despair. But if you allow it to wash over you, if you don't get *stuck* in it, then you can learn what is possible beyond fear. This is why many souls are taking this body trip. There is no way around but through. Then you will see why the trip was necessary.

Breathe into fear wherever you find it in the body. You can breathe it down to nothing. If you focus on the breath as habitual fears surface, they will lose their power to control you. By doing this, you create the space to step back and view them calmly, recognizing that *you* are not the fear.

The paradox is not to be afraid in the presence of fear. Fear is a phantom, but if you believe in it strongly enough, it becomes a powerful pseudo-reality. It's possible to unmask this phantom by going inside to a calmer, deeper place beyond the level of fear. You can both acknowledge the presence of fear and go beyond it, as an airplane goes through a cloud bank. A thunderhead may look solid, but it's possible to pass through it into the sunshine.

When you embrace the dark, you'll notice that much is gestating there. Darkness can be the womb of light; it has its place and its purpose. It will not swallow you, but will surround you like the comfort of the night sky. The stars are no less present on your darkest night. The beginning of the end of fear's dominion is remembering—who you are, where you come from, that you live in the Eternal Now.

You have only to recognize that you are already home.

MAKING FRIENDS WITH YOUR FEAR

Fear is the great prankster. There is never any danger to the part of you that really matters. The hands that hold this book, the body that walks and talks, eats and sleeps is your vehicle in this world, but it is not wholly *you*. The part of you that is beyond time, circumstance and matter is learning the lessons that fear provides, so that it can learn the lessons that love provides.

When fear so overtakes your life that love seems to disappear, remember that this is part of the illusion. Learning about fear is a path to learning about love, and love is why you're here. Love is the essence of where you come from; Love is where you return until there is no more returning. You are an intrinsic and necessary part of Love. Without you, Love would be less than whole, and this is an impossibility.

When fear comes up and runs around you in circles, creating its special kind of madness, this is when you have the opportunity and the privilege to surround it with love, as you'd hold a frightened child in a thunderstorm, singing to her, telling her stories of brave knights and clever ladies. Love is all around you. You could not *be* if you were not in this 'soup' of Love. By loving your fear, by having compassion for it, you help it to move on. Then it no longer runs your life. When fear leaves, your life purpose is revealed by Love.

As you have compassion for your fear, you may notice that it's no more real than a Halloween ghost. Fear cannot prosper in the light. Human beings grow toward their full potential in the light of Love. Allow this big picture to inform the fears that touch your days. Let it provide remembrance, and the courage to sit with fear as it teaches you what is beyond itself. Talk to it, listen to it, and you'll find a freedom you can barely believe.

There is plenty of room to experiment, because there is *plenty*. The fear of not enough—love, money, things, leisure, pleasure—can send you spinning on the wheel of anxiety. But then you have an opportunity to make a choice. Shall I choose something or someone out of fear, inadequacy, a desire to accommodate, or shall I choose from love of self? If I choose out of fear, no harm done in the long run—just another opportunity to observe and experience that fear doesn't work. More precisely: fear works, love plays. Fear inhibits, love frees. Fear hesitates, love leaps into the unknown. Love trusts itself.

BEYOND FEAR TO LOVE AND WISDOM

Can you imagine a life lived from love? No more calculation, holding back or making the 'sensible' decision; no more reasons to be cautious. What would life be like if you lived each moment putting love of self first and trusted that all else would follow? The paradox is that you must first be generous to *your* soul, *your* Self, *your* eternal essence.

Because you are unique, you bring your special gifts to share and lessons to learn. The lessons are often disguised as hardship, pain and fear—especially fear. Fear is one of the most pervasive illusions that humans can experience. It is a hobgoblin that follows you around, often out of habit, even out of a sense of comfort in the familiar. But fear is in your life to be unmasked. Remove fear's mask and you discover the freedom to take a fresh look at who you are beneath the conditioning and the faintheartedness. You are a being of light, one of infinite possibility, even when you temporarily choose finite impossibility.

The price of admission to possibility is leaving fear at the door. Fear is a sneaky old habit, so don't think you're a failure when you find yourself falling into it. Just lay it down again until you get used to traveling without it. At first, such freedom may be disorienting. How much freedom can a human being tolerate! *Human* being is a role you're playing these days. You've played the human part before and you know how to perform it well, but eternal being is your essence.

Living as a child of the Universe, with no bags packed, will bring you to the growing edge of your life and free you from the slavery of fear. Life can be lived without fear as you trust your purpose and use your unique gifts. Then, Spirit takes you seriously and honors your intentions; the reality of Love proclaims itself wherever you are. The Universe is eager to manifest its riches to you, but you must clear away the blocks, one compassionate thought at a time. Your full participation is necessary to change old patterns. Overcoming fear is the breakthrough moment for each human. When enough individual breakthroughs happen, there will be a paradigm shift.

We invite you to take love seriously. It is the simplest and most empowering thing you can do. When you choose to love, you are in perfect safety. The suffering and cruelty in your world makes this truth no less so. Trusting love allows it to reveal itself. Not trusting love prevents you from experiencing it even as you are surrounded by it. And…you are free to forget and remember as many times as you wish. As you choose to put fear aside, to open your heart and love in spite of fear, you will see glimpses of the meta-journey of creation. This is the journey of all created beings, with whatever level of consciousness they have. This is the purpose of all the uncounted universes in the cosmos—to ultimately return to Love.

Making the decision to love is the pre-eminently wise decision. Love-informed action is profound and whole. Your highest wisdom doesn't abandon you in the midst of fearful imaginings. That is impossible, because the wisdom that is your divine heritage is an integral part of you, the part of you beyond circumstance and feeling. This wisdom longs to be expressed through you. There is a part of divine wisdom that can be shared *only* through you, because you are a unique expression of the Divine Self.

If you repress this wisdom, there is a price to be paid. Not a punishment—this isn't how the Universe works—but the outcome can be uncomfortable. The discomfort is a reminder to get on with the deeper purposes of your life. The impetus to right action flows from awareness of your connection to Divine Wisdom. This is the most efficient way to act in your world.

The more you practice listening to your higher self, the more all your experiences become ways for wisdom to reveal itself. It speaks to you through intuition, desire, books, music and art, travel, persons you encounter, through coincidence and synchronicity. But part of becoming wise is a willingness to let go of the process. Instead, allow the wisdom in a situation to reveal itself. Anxiously seeking wisdom ensures that it will elude you. Spirit has a sense of humor, and a ponderous attitude will ensure a side-trip on the journey. Trust the wisdom of your spirit in a childlike way, and act on the promptings of this knowing with confidence. You have the ability to sense integrity and authenticity, and at the deepest level you have the wisdom to discover what you need to know.

Surrendering to this new level of knowing isn't the same as giving your power away; it's about claiming it. It's like the energy in the eye of a great storm. All around is wild wind and chaos—and at the center, peace. Not a passive peace, but a dynamic one that sets the boundaries of the chaos that surrounds it.

When you become the eye of the storm, you claim great power with deep roots that cannot be shaken. Ground yourself by visualizing these roots going down deep into the center of the earth, spreading out as they descend. Stand your ground and experience when it's time to say yes and when to say no. There is a yes from your personality and a yes from your spirit. *This* yes plants those roots in the center of your being. When a yes from the head and the heart concur, that yes has great power.

You have all the resources and wisdom you need to make sound decisions. And if you should make one you later consider unwise, then you have the opportunity to reflect back on what the lessons were in this situation. All that happens serves to bring you to the next level of understanding. This insight gives you the freedom to act fearlessly, knowing in the larger sense that there are no mistakes, just opportunities to fine tune your developing wisdom.

Trust your deepest knowing; act from a place of love for yourself and others. Remember that your Path is protected, from the beginning of beginnings. Can you see how this reassurance can allow your courage to blaze forth?

THE ULTIMATE FEAR—TRANSITION TO SPIRIT

My mother was afraid to die. She had been programmed to believe that the best that might await her in the afterlife was an unknown number of years in purgatory. I think this is why she lived so long, even though she was very unhappy those last years. She always said she would be carried out of her house feet first, and that's exactly what happened. The night that she was to suffer a stroke, my son Chris brought dinner up to her room, where she was reading the evening paper. After he left, she had a massive cerebral bleed. Before she lost consciousness, she scribbled a note to Chris as he came upstairs to collect her tray. She wrote—I love you. This was her last communication. She died in the local hospital a few hours later.

As I kept vigil by her bedside, I sensed that she was being helped across the divide between what we think of as life and death. Although she was in a profound coma, twice she sat up and attempted to speak with whomever she seemed to see at the foot of her bed. She died a few minutes later.

Death is the experience most feared, and yet integral to human experience. It is not the end of life, not annihilation nor cessation of experience, or worse, the beginning of punishment—all notions humans have believed in tenaciously.

The fear of death can be overcome completely only by dying, and remembering then what it's all about. Death is a transition that evokes great terror among many of you.

We are experts on this subject, having gone through it so many times! You are, too, but you have agreed to forget so that you can learn the lessons inherent in overcoming fear. When fear is finally overcome, there's no longer a need to return to a body—unless you choose to out of love.

What is this passage called death? Where do you go when you die? What happens when you get there? The answers to these questions are not the same for everyone. There are as many kinds of death as there are souls who experience it. You will have exactly the kind of death you need—and we say this lovingly. Death can be joyous, or it can be confusing or frightening, if you insist. It's a step on the Path, a passage to the next level of learning, or an opportunity to rest awhile and try again.

Sometimes death is a compassionate gift to a person whose body is wearing out or experiencing intractable pain. Even if it comes when your companions can't make sense of such an untimely departure—to the soul, death always happens at the right time. Only your spirit knows when its tasks are accomplished. From this point of view, the deaths of children, or accidental deaths, are not the tragedies they seem.

When a loved one dies, you see only a lifeless body, but the soul continues on its journey until there are no more lessons to be learned, no more return trips necessary. It is the *transition* from life in a body to life in spirit, this great unknown experience, that humans fear. It's especially important to lovingly remind one who is about to return to spirit that there is nothing to fear, ever. Great help surrounds each one making this transition.

When you say goodbye to your beloveds at death, you're really wishing them 'til we meet again.' Certainly there is grieving for the loss of their physical presence, but the loss is an illusion, and a temporary one. Those left behind miss the comfort of the senses—the touch, the voice, the sight of the one who has passed on—but the connection with your loved ones endures.

What seems impossible is not only possible, it is the journey each soul agrees to make; to remember again and again that you are beloved beings, held eternally in existence by the animating principle of the universe we name Love. Everyone not only participates in this love force, but ultimately returns to it.

All strivings, struggle and ego conflicts are ultimately fleeting. What is lasting and incapable of corruption is the existence of spirit, which transcends the body even while part of it. Evidence of the spirit's survival of the body's death is everywhere, if your heart is open to see.

The human journey is full of seductive diversions. This is the nature of being in a body. As you walk the Path, you come to see these distractions for what they are, and as your spirit prepares to move on, you let them go. Releasing life as it's lived in a body is unique to each soul. It is the quintessential journey of spirit infused in flesh.

You and your loved ones are eternally safe, especially as you move on to spirit. Not only are all your journeys guided, you are on a trajectory back to Love. Nothing can harm the essence of anyone. Even human disasters in which thousands 'lose their lives' in floods, earthquakes and war, are only illusions of danger. These souls are carried along on the stream of life. Death is the way humans explain the transition to life in spirit. The one who has crossed over sees a new vista, old friends, or takes needed rest before continuing on the Path.

Do we therefore count death as nothing? Nothing is emptiness, a void. Death is a passage from one state of being to another. We don't imply that grief and tears are inappropriate. Feelings expressed from the heart are always appropriate; human loss and grief are experiences of being in a body.

Be open to all of life, including the mystery of death. There is never anything to fear that happens in or beyond your physical life. To learn at the moment of death that you are not dead, but gloriously safe and alive, is joy and blessed relief to the soul. If you still need reassurance, we remind you of the reports of many persons who have had near-death experiences. For them, the closeness to the presence of Love and Light has, once and for all, dispelled any fear of death. Again we remind you—you are eternally safe and loved. We encourage you to suspend your doubt and live your life as if you believe this.

◦◦

My best friend has been diagnosed with terminal cancer. Is there something she needs to learn from this illness? How can I best help her?

Illness is always an opportunity to let go of fear; a reminder that everyone is completely safe in this creation. We know this way of thinking offends the mind. Mind wants to know the answers, particularly about impending bad news. This soul of whom you speak has her unique lessons to learn here. Trust that she is doing the work she has signed up for. Though it may seem to defy common sense, on a soul level, she has chosen these particular lessons for this lifetime.

We don't say that healing is impossible. We do say that her illness is an opportunity. The idea that illness, particularly cancer, could be a gift, unsettles those who like to figure things out and live as if they're in control of life.

Illness, in spite of what it may seem, is an outer event. So your friend is in no danger, healed or dead. Her essence, the part of her that you call her soul, will know if her work here is complete this time around. Her personality may not know. It may not even want to bring this soul issue into the light of her conscious mind. But the agenda of her spirit will be accomplished, even if her mind resists knowing.

You can best help by sending her your love. A lesson for you is to lovingly let her go. This doesn't necessarily mean good-bye—and ultimately, good-byes are temporary. She is held in the love of the Beloved. This is what eternal safety is all about.

Courage—The Walk of the Warrior

In ancient times, warriors asked to be surrounded by the protection of the gods. They put on the raiment of war—helmet, chain mail. They carried a shield and a sword. Now, preparing for challenging experiences helps you to see fear as the phantom it is, because you cannot 'die' in your battles. They are encounters your soul has agreed to. Some humans need to go through fear and upheaval on the way to fearlessness and peace. Others are learning all they need to know about fear. For them, overcoming fear makes room for courage.

Healing Your Fear

It's possible to be both loving and a warrior, but it's not always easy. You start by loving and honoring yourself, your unique journey and your purpose for being here in physical form. Your mind doesn't have to figure it all out; your spirit knows and remembers.

Your life is perfect as it is right now. It's perfect for you on your unique Path. Challenges appear because you've asked for them on a soul level. You've agreed that you're ready to take them on in a gracious surrender to the wisdom and beauty of your Path and your tasks on the Path.

Courage makes choices in the presence of fear. It acknowledges fear but isn't shackled by it. Courage honors the agenda of your spirit. It accompanies warriors on the Path. They clothe themselves with the garments of protection, but if they should appear to die on the battlefield, in spite of shield and sword, they step out of the shell of their bodies and walk on.

You might think—it's easy for *them* to say there is nothing to fear, but this is the truth we want so passionately to share with you. Courage comes as you step out on the Path, one protected footfall at a time.

Healing Your Fear

~⊚~

A friend asks the Committee about health concerns.

Our dear one,

First we reiterate—there is nothing to fear. This is the primary lesson, and we understand the challenges of being in a body that is vulnerable—always changing, always growing older. But you are never abandoned, ever, on this journey. Everything that happens is for your learning, for your growth in consciousness. This doesn't mean that you surrender to your body's illnesses; it means that you hold them in the larger context of the work you've agreed to do this time around.

As you observe the state of your planet, it's easy to become disillusioned, to wonder if there *is* a grand plan of overarching love. Does this Being whose essence is love care about your blood pressure? Does It care about the wars in the Middle East and the ethnic cleansings in Africa? We understand these days that faith requires courage, as it has in every era. Your species is one that often chooses to grow through pain, to learn its lessons the hard way, or so it appears. All the illness, cruelty, the apparent madness in the world, the craze for power—all is grist for this patient honing of the heart toward Love. Love is exquisitely eternally patient as fear is transformed into love.

We encourage you therefore to hold the awareness of being part of this great Love. When you live from this place, death is experienced as illusion. Living this way requires attention, focus, and a commitment to ignore the symptoms, the bad news, all the distractions that lure you into forgetting. And the secret is bringing the attention back to the present moment. Then what is essential becomes clear; what is peripheral more easily slips away.

When you make decisions from *this* place—about the health of your body, about how you choose to spend your time, about the thoughts you allow in—life becomes more balanced and simple. Such focus is not easy to maintain. It's the challenge of life in a body. But you and others like you are being invited to participate in this experiment in the evolution of consciousness. It's a privilege to be in a body at this time.

4

A Journey Through Fear

You are in no danger—ever.

In 2003, the Committee guided me through an ongoing heart problem. I would be relaxing in the evening, reading in my favorite chair; or I might wake from a sound sleep in the middle of the night as my heart rate would accelerate from normal to 200 or more beats per minute. After several months, the problem was corrected by a procedure called ablation. I'm enormously grateful that I live in an era in which such a sophisticated intervention is available, and I'm happy to report that I've returned to excellent health.

February 27

Late last night, after frightening symptoms persisted for several hours, a friend drove me to the emergency room of a large medical center an hour away from home. Snow was falling lightly as we drove down the highway. It was the beginning of a blizzard that would continue the next day. In spite of efforts to breathe deeply and practice what the Committee has been teaching me, I was in full-blown fear, fantasizing about the possibility of stroke or heart attack. I was admitted for three days of tests.

L et us start with our mantra—you are in no danger, ever. You are doing all the right things to protect your health. The rest is daring, in the face of fear, to claim what you know. Faith is a suspension of reason, a leap into the unknown. But if you *know* what is true, beyond faith or belief, this can be a major step in your spiritual development.

You are here in this place of duality to learn and prosper.

Your work here is not done. You cannot leave until it is. There was and is purpose in this lifetime. You are no random accident in this place of being. You have chosen to be here at this time to learn and to share what you're learning.

Today you are learning about compassion for yourself and others, and still more about patience. Our dear one, the lessons don't have to be difficult. Accepting fully your 'assignment' will greatly ease the way.

March 31

I ask about the meaning of my scary symptoms.

We remind you again that you're never in any danger. You are held in Love, when you remember and when you forget. The Beloved, by its very nature, can only love. It is in this context of being loved that we ask you to view your physical challenges. One of the reasons you have them is that you've signed up to be a human being, to have a body that gets sick, is able to heal and ultimately dies. But your body is not who you are. You are as eternal as the One in whose nature you share. When you remember who you are, you can best learn the lessons your symptoms are teaching you.

You are here to expand your awareness so that you become *conscious* of your Divinity. You see the results all around you of those who behave as if they have no share in Divinity. The consequences are hard to look at—innocents suffering and dying, decisions made to kill and maim in the name of freedom. True freedom comes when you know who you are—beyond time and physical circumstance.

What does all this have to do with your racing heart? You are now in an intense learning place; one your spirit has sought beyond the preferences of your personality. This is a time for opening your heart. It will not break in the process, and we say this knowing these irregularities are a strain on your body. You have agreed to be a teacher here, and teachers need to experience what they teach.

'Internalize' is a word we've heard you use with your students. *You* are a student now, in order to learn what is true in your very being—in your cells, in your blood, in your heart beating. You are in the school of compassion. You can't have it for others if you don't have it for yourself. You can share only who you are. This is the curriculum you must internalize in order to teach others.

Part of what you're learning is how to release fear when it comes up. But first you must discover what it is and what it isn't, because unexamined fear has power. Turning your back on it, denying it or pretending it's not there doesn't work. You have to look fear in the face and say: "I am here and I am real. *I* am an eternal being, a sharer in the Divine, and *you* are a phantom created in my imagination. You have served me well in the past, but now I don't need you anymore, and I release you."

Learning to release fear is the content of your and everyone's master class, because in order to be a master, you must first let go of fear. The sooner you can do this, the sooner your body will adjust to a new level of functioning. This time is a gift and an opportunity for growth. Do all that seems appropriate to bring your body into balance. At the same time, learn why you're out of balance and why this shifting is necessary.

April 29

By now, I have become a regular customer in the emergency

room of the small hospital close to home. The doctors are still trying to figure out what's going on.

We greet you in the midst of your challenges. It is true that we are your loving guides, but this is the time for you to become your own teacher. We can guide, support and encourage, but you must step out. As you now know, the earth plane is not for the fainthearted. You learn what you need to learn by practicing patience, compassion, and courage. You know the root of the word courage is from the French for heart, *coeur*. You're being asked to practice heart lessons on many levels.

You may have to experience fear along the way to discover that it is illusion. The invitation is to walk through the door of illusion into the Light. On the other side of fear, Love always waits.

Truth doesn't change because life circumstances become frightening. But it's wise to practice in small easy ways to prepare yourself when bigger challenges come. The process is always the same: open your heart and step out on the Path, one footfall, one breath at a time. You are not alone as you do this. Whether you feel it or not, guidance and love surround you.

May 8

A diagnosis has finally been made, but none of the several medications that the cardiologist has prescribed relieve my racing heart. I've learned about a high-tech procedure that could repair my heart, so my family and I have decided that I should go ahead with this option, scheduled for the end of May.

We acknowledge the challenges that these days hold for you. Especially now, you are held in the love of Spirit. This is what it means to be human—you sign up for the school of Love. And in order to learn about it, you experience what it is not—fear, disappointment, regret about apparently missed opportunities, poor judgment, illness, betrayal. When you've had enough, a door opens in your heart and you walk into the presence of Love.

The reality is that Love has been with you always. You get distracted by all of life's experiences, including the good ones. *They* delude you into thinking you have enough love, good luck or success, until you remember the one essential thing—that you are part of this great Love that is of your very essence. In the moment when you consciously choose to be in Love's presence, life changes forever. This is what the mystics of all spiritual traditions have discovered. It doesn't matter if your physical heart is ailing or if you're about to be burned at the stake. *It doesn't matter!* Because you remember that you are Love.

Each soul has its lives to live, with its many experiences, before each one comes to this door. It's a door of knowledge beyond facts or research; a door of experience beyond any temporal circumstance. Walking through this door catapults you into being. Then, whether you're healthy, prosperous, wise or even alive is unimportant. You remember who you are.

May 14

My symptoms continue to show up unexpectedly. Now I'm on a thirty day monitor that automatically alerts the cardiologist on call when my heart rate accelerates. I continue to practice what the Committee teaches and the techniques my doctors have suggested, but when my body flies out of control, all my old fears kick in. I've done a lot of inner listening and spiritual reading and it's helped. I feel as if I'm in an accelerated spiritual curriculum.

The procedure soon to be performed on your heart will not harm you. It will ease the symptoms, and though important, this is but one step in your full healing. Your symptoms have been at the least distracting and at the worst terrifying, as they have kept attention focused on your body. Your focus needs to be all inclusive. Feel your feelings, use your intelligence to advocate for your best care, *and* be in communication with your spirit. It is this part of you that goes beyond feelings, intelligence and strategy. Your spirit guides you to uncover your purpose here, the reasons you've returned this time, in these circumstances. It reminds you that you are safe and cherished in this place of duality in which you have chosen to learn and grow.

When you have learned the essentials and experience the truth beyond duality, then you finally 'get it.' And when you know in this experiential way, then you can share that knowing, which is beyond belief, with others who are ready to hear.

This doesn't mean that fear disappears. It means that you

learn to make it an ally. Fear reminds you to go beyond itself to a place of peace and love where you experience that it has no power unless *you* give it power.

This illness is an opportunity for integration, so that you can do the work you're here to do. This process can be a joyful one. Hold your heart lovingly as it's in the process of being repaired. These symptoms will not kill your body. They are part of the plan you've chosen. Don't resist them. Work with them. Help them to move along. It's possible to do all that needs to be done in these days. Trust the process.

May 18, in the local hospital

Earlier today, my son Justin arrived at my home after a long drive. Tomorrow we were planning to attend a family graduation several hours away. I'm scheduled for an ablation in ten days, but I had been feeling fine, so I was confident I'd be able to make the trip.

Suddenly, my heart started to race, and I knew that I needed to go to the emergency room. This time, the ER doctor decided to admit me. I was terribly disappointed to miss our family celebration, and discouraged that I couldn't count on my body to behave itself.

I've been assigned to a four bed room. The fear in this room is palpable, especially from a young Hispanic woman who speaks no English and is about to have emergency gall bladder surgery.

We are here with you. This is an opportunity to practice, practice, practice: to remember that you are safe in the midst of all the medical apparatus, and others' illness and fear. The Beloved is present wherever your physical body happens to be.

Rest in Spirit's love; remember that you are a cherished child of creation. Without you the cosmos would be incomplete. This is not grandiosity, it's reality, and you are no more or less special than any other soul. Each one is necessary—in its sufferings, its breakthroughs, even its banalities. Each soul walks a unique path on the way to uncovering the Self. Your soul is no less present because it is disguised, or because some don't believe in its reality; it is no less real through sickness and the eventual shedding of the body.

Your indestructible eternal essence is present through all

the soul's adventures. No circumstance has the power to separate you from it. Until you *know* this reality—not just believe or wish it to be true, but *experience* it—nothing else we say makes sense.

This is reality: you come from Love; you are an essential, unique, indivisible part of that Love, and you are destined ultimately to return to it. Sink into this reality with every breath. This is your assignment.

May 22

After five days of tests at the local hospital, I was transferred yesterday by ambulance (insisting unsuccessfully that I was well enough to go by car) to a major medical center where the previously scheduled procedure date has been pushed up to tomorrow. I was anxious, but also encouraged because I knew that I was in the most skilled hands at this highly regarded teaching hospital. I also felt a sense of inner peace and safety that could only be a gift from Spirit.

Today you get to learn even more about fear! And you thought you knew all there was to know and were ready to let it go once and for all—the big letting go of fear that finally makes room for Love. But there is one piece of business left to do. You must love fear before you can let it go. Don't try to banish it to the outer darkness, don't allow yourself to feel superior to it or beyond it, don't deal with it by ignoring it—you know where *that* strategy can lead. It is a paradox, perhaps the ultimate one: *you must love fear before you can leave it behind.* And you must be grateful to it for the good things it has done for you—pushing you to go deeper into understanding and keeping you out of physical danger.

Are you willing at last to hold fear in your arms, as you would a sleepy child whom you love? This is the way to conquer fear—by loving it away. Give it a loving send-off to its proper place in the cosmos. Then your heart will fill with love because nature abhors a vacuum. In this way, you become compassionate both to the fear and to those who have difficulty letting it go, including you.

June 6

It's been two weeks since the procedure. I'm back home recovering nicely, with only a little residual tiredness. In the electrophysiology lab, where the procedure took place, I woke up in time to see the medical team celebrate their success by high-fiving each other.

It's time for you to understand that you are your own teacher. We don't say this because we're abandoning you. How could we leave you? You are of our very being. We encourage you to trust the deep well of this experience you have called to yourself. Trust the knowledge and intuition that is your heritage, as an expression in time of the One, the Source, the All That Is, the Creator, God, Goddess—all words that attempt to describe the ineffable.

Everyone comes to this place of duality with all the resources required to break through the illusion of separation. You arrive with this innate knowing embedded in your soul and in your genetic makeup. All your ancestors, back to the very beginning of your species, have prepared the way for you to know in this unique way, even as you prepare the way for those who follow to know in a way that builds on *your* access to Spirit. This is a natural process that may seem glacially slow, but it's perfect in its way. Knowing comes through silence and expectant listening.

Every human comes equipped with this capability. It's standard issue, not a perk for the ascetic.

Part of your purpose here is to show the way for others to trust *their* intuition, to know *their* truth. Truth is not as easily found in temples, mosques and cathedrals, as those who are the custodians of these places would have you believe. The knowledge you need for your journey is found in the quiet place of your unique expression of Spirit, but you must be still and make space for the listening. Spirit will not intrude; it will nudge, but not come crashing in.

The nudges are invitations from Love to explore the reality of who you are—to find the way through fear to the other side where Love waits. Where Love is, there is no 'other side,' but humans create the 'here' and 'there' out of illusion, and as we love to say, you are here to break through illusion once and for all.

June 11

I'm having uncomfortable symptoms while I am healing— my heart often pounds forcefully. I can almost hear it as well as feel it. (I learned later that this symptom was a normal part of the healing process.)

The difficulties you are experiencing are not cause for you to 'lose heart.' We are teasing you a little about these symptoms to remind you that everything that happens you've called to yourself, in a way that's part of the perfect plan to uncover who you *really* are, beneath the disguise of your personality and your healing body. This process is allowing you the space and time to go within. And we understand, you often find nothing there but chatter. Nevertheless, the practice of quieting the mind is a way to discover how your life in this body relates to the bigger picture.

There is nothing to fear in these days. Soon this time will be seen as a precious gift of Spirit. You are learning to be loving and compassionate to yourself. It's way past time to let go of self-judgment. It's time to embrace your existence as an expression of Spirit slowed down in time. This is everyone's heritage, one they will ultimately recognize and claim. Evolution to greater consciousness is moved forward by each soul who progresses from unconscious to conscious spirit. Once you know who you are, you can never *not* know again, at least in *this* incarnation. Knowing means the old game is up. God can no longer be seen as an angry patriarch who punishes sin.

Continue to be open to what your heart lessons are teaching you. But remember, you can't learn in fear. When fear shows up, send it gently on its way. Then your heart can reveal to you what you are ready to see.

June 25

More heart pounding this evening. I'm getting discouraged. Do I have still more to learn about overcoming fear?

Your discomfort is an opportunity for you to trust your purpose. We know the pounding brings up fear again, your old nemesis. Fear is more like a worthy adversary than an enemy. Do you think you've called these feelings to yourself for no purpose? The Universe doesn't treat its beloved beings whimsically. It provides them with all the opportunities they need to fulfill their agreement with Love. Every created being has an agenda for each incarnation. If the pressure seems revved up these days, it's because you're able to internalize more truth.

Can you choose to regard your symptoms as the beginning of the end of your journey in this body? Of course. You can view the 'end' of your life as a tragedy, a looming catastrophe to be put off as long as possible, or as an opportunity for new growth and adventure. Or you can choose to view these symptoms as an opportunity for deeper learning. You purposefully choose every event and every encounter that happens to you. You are everlastingly protected, and your purpose in this incarnation will be realized before you leave.

What is that purpose? As we remind you again and again, it is to become who you are most completely, most magnificently, and to teach others to do the same. You are a teacher by instinct and training, and you have more to accomplish. There is really nothing to do beyond remembering that you're on the Path—and the way will be shown, one step at a time. You need to release being in charge of the whole journey. Our dear one, the tickets to where you're going have been pre-paid.

August 6,

My recovery is complete. Tomorrow I see Nancy, my

acupuncturist, whose treatments through these months have been a huge help, both energetically and physically. I have so much to be grateful for, including a newly repaired heart to take with me on my journey.

This is a time to consciously become aware of all that you know, to integrate your knowledge and your intuition. It's a time to tie together all the strands of truth we've been teaching you, and that your higher self has been revealing. There is really nothing new to learn. Knowing comes through the mind, but is more than mind. This intuitive knowledge of reality is your birthright as co-creator of your life. Universal truths are elegant in their simplicity: reality is Love; each human is a manifestation in time of Love incarnated in a body, mind and spirit. Everyone is here by conscious choice to learn again that this is so.

Beyond knowing and remembering, you have chosen to come to this place of duality with all its beauty and pain, to demonstrate—by the way you live, by the choices you make—that you *know* what is real and what is illusion. Even though you sometimes forget, and can be seduced by the drama around you, you then remember once again that you are eternal spirit temporarily masquerading as a human.

When life in the body is especially wonderful, the pleasures of being in the world can cause you to forget who you are as readily as the pain. Pain is a reminder to be in each moment, trusting your purpose. Your life here is to be enjoyed but not held tightly. There is nothing new to learn. Knowing comes through the mind, but is more than mind. This intuitive knowledge of reality is your birthright as co-creator of your life.

5

The Illusion of Evil

*All evil can be reduced to fear that judges harshly.
This is how the absence of love shows itself.*

Evil is a forgetting of your true nature. The essence of every human is love, including those who deny who they are by behaving unlovingly. Behavior that seems so clearly immoral and lacking in good will is like self-hypnosis to the person acting this way. When love is denied, the result may look like evil, even madness. It's a challenge to see those acting from denial of love as manifestations of Spirit, but an unshakable belief in each soul's essence can help you to cope with the painful consequences of this forgetting.

How can you respond when you're in the midst of evil? One strategy is to play the game of spiritual Tai Chi. This is a way of stepping aside to deflect the blows sent your way. Another strategy is to consciously surround yourself with the power of Love. This may sound abstract, but we assure you, it is not. The energy of Love is real; it is doubt that prevents you from experiencing it. Doubt is *the* human condition to be overcome. Respond in these new ways in spite of your doubt. Act as if there were no doubt. Even the greatest cynic, or a believer in the reality of evil, can choose a loving response in the presence of forgetting. You can even do it as a kind of experiment, out of intellectual curiosity. What matters is that you change your response.

All evil can be reduced to fear that judges harshly. This is how the absence of love shows itself. When you resist evil, you set up an adversarial position between good and evil that gives evil power. Instead, recognize evil as fear, and assuage it with love. Common wisdom says this is a misguided way to respond; some might call it massive denial of reality. But we challenge you to love in the presence of evil.

Each soul has its unique journey through the thickets of judgment and fear. Everyone continues to fear until the illusion is unmasked. Surround the person consumed by fear with love, and trust unwaveringly in the wisdom of that soul's essence. Living through such experiences is the primary school of love. Graduation to the next level reveals yet another universe of lessons—and on and on as the soul sheds all that is not love. At the center, finally, is Love, revealed to be you and us and everyone.

Sometimes, doing nothing in the face of evil equals condoning it, and colludes in the forgetting. When Jesus kicked out the money changers from the temple, this act was accomplished with the boldness of a warrior. Great strength comes from clarity of intention. If you must act with such strength, Spirit will guide you to the appropriate *and* loving action.

Don't be invested in a particular or immediate outcome. Your response is no less valid if the 'evil doer' doesn't seem to change. You may not be aware of the levels on which your response is affecting another. Don't worry about changing anyone else. More important is how your response affects *you*. Surround yourself with light in the presence of apparent evil, and use your intuition to steer you away from its presence as much as possible. Some encounters you *choose* in order to learn. When the lesson is learned, the issue no longer need appear in your life.

Humans often wonder why the world seems full of violence. Earth is a place of polarity and paradox. The earth experience teaches humans about the nature of duality. When a soul has had enough of these lessons, when it finally understands that duality is a grand illusion, then school is out forever.

Meanwhile, the illusion in the presence of danger is that you're not safe. You are afraid that you might 'die' as a result of evil; that your loved ones might suffer or that war might break out. These events do happen in the context of the world's illusion, but no one is ever in danger; no one dies in your sense of that word. Suffering, no matter how intense, cannot harm the core of anyone.

The magnificent and sometimes harsh earth is a way station to greater reality. You are here to remember that love, joy and creativity are reality; that hatred, cruelty and greed are illusion. Holding the frightening events of your world in the frame of eternal safety is the most effective way to change them. They can be changed only by a shift in human consciousness, and each human who doesn't buy into fear affects the entire pool of consciousness. We do not exaggerate. Every soul is critical at this accelerating time in human evolution. Yet, from another perspective, there's no hurry. Everything happens at the perfect time.

In the midst of your concerns for the world, we challenge you to decline to join the chorus of worriers and doomsayers. Your role, as is the role of all who strive to live in the Light, is to surround frightening, apparently evil events with *your* light. In this way you become an active peacemonger—we suggest such a word as an antidote to all the warmongering. Join with like-hearted souls to make a happy ruckus for peace. No peace movement succeeds that comes from righteous indignation or anger. Literally love your enemies. This is the most efficient way to ensure their defeat.

No injustice has any power to harm you. Nothing that happens in the world can touch your indestructible essence. Injustice may impinge on your comfort or offend your principles; it may even make inroads into your bank account—but all these circumstances are outer events.

Take a break from the world's turmoil and go inside to a place of peace and rest. This place is no less real when you focus on grievances. How much outrage are you willing to live with? With an act of will, you can move to the peace at your center. Breathe yourself down into this space. It will renew your spirit and illumine the way.

You always have the option to view evil as part of the world's illusion. There is nothing to fear even when it appears that evil has triumphed. What is true cannot be paraded as delusion. What is just cannot remain hidden. Your job is to maintain *your* integrity in the presence of duplicity. The more you recognize the good in everyone, the more it can reveal itself.

The Illusion of Evil

AFTER SEPTEMBER 11, 2001

September 12

On a human level these events are tragic, and evoke a sense of helplessness, anger and great grieving. Upheaval and confusion of this magnitude is new in the experience of those who live in the United States. We don't minimize this death and destruction, *and*, we say to you lovingly, with the greatest respect for your emotions, that there is much more going on than eyes can see and ears can hear.

There is a great chorus of welcome for those who have crossed over into spirit, grand reunions and rejoicing, and some confusion as well. It is difficult for many to leave the body so abruptly. These souls are especially cared for in order to gentle them into spirit.

Each one of you is where you're supposed to be, and we acknowledge how hard this is for minds to fathom. Everyone—including the terrorists—is on the Path, some kicking and screaming, but nonetheless there.

Now is a time to open your hearts to those who are grieving and to those whose bodies have been injured. These are challenging times in which you have chosen to be on the earth. Now is a special opportunity to practice compassion; to send love to those who are hurt and grieving in a way that expects nothing in return. If you believe this makes no difference, we simply share with you what we know—it makes an enormous difference for them and for you.

September 18

A week after this human tragedy, the good news is that so many on the planet have opened themselves to Spirit, and stand in the humble realization that the body, with all its insistent needs and desires, is not to be taken too seriously. This is not to say that there isn't important work that, paradoxically, can be done only in a body. Having a body is a special assignment, but it's just one assignment among many for your soul. The body is a frame, a context in which to do the work of Spirit. It is fragile, as you have been so profoundly reminded. This frame can be broken or burned beyond recognition—and, it is only the frame, the binding of the book, not the story to be told.

Spirit is alive and well in this place of duality. In the aftermath of this violence, humans have expressed love for one another and acknowledged their vulnerability. The human spirit is resilient, and Spirit, of which each person is an indispensable part, is indestructible.

It may strain credulity to acknowledge that extremists who hate America are also part of Spirit, no matter how misguided their minds or closed their hearts. Without them, the plan of creation would be less than it is—another impossibility. Bombarding these militants with love—just love, with no strings attached—is the way to shake their fundamentalist beliefs. Their holy wars thrive on the perceived hatred of their enemies.

This stance is qualitatively different from turning the other cheek. It is not accommodation or capitulation. It is a decision to stand in the power of Love; to send it out to those you mistrust and fear. There can no longer be the luxury of hatred and intolerance. The challenge, as well as the paradox, is to love in the presence of hatred. Confront each thought of hatred with one of love.

Now, as humans are becoming more conscious, you can

more easily practice non-personal love—love that is simply sent out to go where it needs to go. This love has no agenda; it seeks nothing for itself. Think of it like the warmth of the sun that shines on all who stand under a cloudless sky. The sun doesn't differentiate between worthy and unworthy. It warms all in its path.

In the same way, you can send love even to those your mind judges undeserving. This kind of love is an act of will that has nothing to do with your feelings. It is the opposite of being 'in love,' when emotion sent and received is *very* personal. To send such supra-personal love, it is necessary only to open your heart and suspend judgment. Judgment is not your business, nor is blame, or assigning guilt. Your 'job,' if you choose it, is to surround with love those filled with hatred.

Practicing this kind of love nurtures your awareness of Spirit. Spirit loves all of creation simply because it exists, for the sheer joy of it, because Spirit is Love and cannot act contrary to its nature. Loving your perceived enemies allows your spirit to become aligned with a Love so vast its power holds all creation in existence. Sometimes, you can *feel* this love as you send it out; at other times it may seem like a sterile exercise. The *awareness* of your heart opening is a gift, but your personal feelings do not affect the love sent.

This love energy has the power to change the course of Earth's history, and in this era it is possible to accomplish such a change. Now is a potential turning point in the consciousness of Earth, an opportunity not to be missed. It *is* possible that loving can become a habit to replace judgment, suspicion and hatred. And this turning to Love happens one decision at a time, one soul at a time.

By your nature as spirit living in a body, you participate in duality. In the old model of reality, you decide who is right and wrong; who are the villains and the heroes. Humans long for the reassurance of unambiguous polarity and simple explanations, but the life force is much more complex. Terrorists are expressions of Spirit, as are each of you who reads these words. This doesn't excuse the actions of those who kill and destroy. But *your* role is not to destroy the destroyer.

What might happen if you didn't accept the belief that

terrorists were evil? What if you saw instead the Love at the center of their souls? The terrorists who chose to commit violence on September 11 did so out of misguided zeal. Now they are learning how their actions affected so many. They are feeling the grief of the bereaved and the fear of those whose sense of security has been violated. They feel, on a psychic level, the pain of the wounded. They're learning about compassion, tolerance, and love for those they hated. They're facing the consequences of their acts. This is different from punishment; it's more like an intense revelation.

Some of your ancestors were sure that hanging witches and burning heretics at the stake was justifiable. In *this* era, there is an opportunity for a new paradigm of human behavior. It does not start at the top levels of government. It begins at the grassroots, in the behavior of 'ordinary' people. Remember that great ones were also ordinary—carpenters, peasants, cooks, fishermen.

Each of you is important in the global turning toward compassion. Be patient as you explore the complexities of 'good' and 'evil.' Hold *all* extremists in the light of Love, including their leaders, who are so sure they know what is just and unjust.

THE MAN IN THE RED BANDANNA

Welles Crowther was a talented, handsome 24 year old; a young man on the way up. He had been a popular student at Boston College, a varsity lacrosse player. He was employed as an equities trader at Sandler O'Neill, whose offices were in the South Tower of the World Trade Center. Welles shared his first apartment in Greenwich Village with a friend. On Sunday evening, September 9, 2001, he met his parents for dinner in Manhattan. As he pulled a red bandanna out of his back pocket, his mom, Alison, teased him about it. He had picked up the habit of carrying a bandanna from his dad, who used to say, "One for show, and one for blow."

On the morning of September 11, the sky lobby on the 78th floor of the South Tower of the World Trade Center was crowded with workers. Even after the North Tower had been struck by a plane, workers had been assured that *their* building was safe. But many decided to leave anyway, in spite of harassment by some of their colleagues who thought they should remain at their desks. Ling Young, a tax auditor for the state of New York, was among those waiting to board an elevator when the South Tower was hit. She was thrown across the floor by the force of the blast. When she came to, she realized she was badly burned. The soot and smoke was so thick it was hard to see. Ms Young made an effort to clean her glasses which were covered with blood. Suddenly, she heard an authoritative voice saying, "If you can move, follow me." An African-American woman nearby was too dazed to walk. A tall young man picked her up and carried her on his back. A middle-aged Caucasian man appeared disoriented. The voice encouraged, "Stay with me. I've found a stairway." The young man escorted Ms Young and others down to the 61st floor where the air was clear, then said, "I'm going back upstairs to help." Judy Wein was also in the sky lobby when the second plane struck. She suffered a broken arm, a punctured lung and several cracked ribs. She heard someone say, "If you can walk, please follow me." The voice belonged to a man who had tied a red bandanna across his mouth and nose. He stayed with Ms Wein and several others for about 15 flights. Then he turned and headed back up the stairs, determined to make another try.

In March of 2002, Welles Crowther's body was found in what had been the lobby of the South Tower, at the firefighters' command center. He had made it out safely, but chose to stay on and help. Johnny Howells, Welles's college roommate, said, "Sometimes I wish he didn't do the right thing; that he came out alive instead, but then that just wouldn't be Welles." In May, Ling Young and Judy Wein were interviewed by the New York Times. They described the handsome young man with the red bandanna who had led them and many others to safety on the morning of 9/11. Alison Crowther read the article and knew immediately that these women were describing her son. She met Ms Young and Ms Wein soon afterwards in what one can only imagine was a meeting filled with both grief and gratitude.

The Illusion of Evil

On October 3, 2001 the Committee gave a message to Alison Crowther:

We would say this, our dear one—it is inconceivable to the mind that love can prevail over death. And yet, we assure you, Love is all that prevails. The rest is all transient, as you know now so intimately and painfully—the personality, the body that seems so solid, the head full of ideas and dreams.

What is real, but beyond our ability to prove to you in a concrete way, is that your son is alive and well today. He is recovering, along with so many companions, from the shock and surprise of being catapulted into spirit. He and all the others who 'died' together on that day are learning (it's more like remembering) what it's like to live without a body. Your son and his companions in this new adventure are free of sadness. They are remembering again what it's like to be fully in spirit, and it feels like a homecoming.

All created beings, with or without bodies, are where they are to learn what they need in order to move on to the next level of their development—we no less than any of you. And where are we all heading? Where does this learning lead? It leads to the uncovering of the Love which is at the heart of all our beings—which connects us to God, Allah, the Source—whatever names you choose to personify Love. It is from this all-encompassing Love that you have come, and it is to this Love that you ultimately return. Each of you is an indispensable part of Love; without you it would be less faceted, less multi-dimensional.

Do you see how important each soul is? How each adds a little glory and its own uniqueness to the whole? The adventures along the way—the birthings and the transitions into spirit, whether in infancy, in the flowering of young adulthood or in old age, all have within them the opportunities each soul needs on its way to the Light. And there is no hurry. Love is infinitely patient.

We reassure you that your beloved son is safe. He is being cared for during this transition by many loving beings, some of whom he recognizes with great delight. He assures you that he is on the Path, on his journey, as are all of you, his beloveds. There is no fear where he is; there is respite and companionship, so that all these transitions into spirit are accomplished as compassionately as possible.

Those you love are never lost to you. From all places of being, love continues to flow.

Alison asks: What was Welles's experience as he was dying in the Tower?

The transition between states of being that you label death is more like the process of waking from sleep, or from a deep dream in which the waking state is at first disorienting. You may ask after such an intense dream: Where am I? or even, Who am I? The awakening from physical life is similar. Every spirit has the death experience it needs to make the most useful transition for its ongoing development. That's the big picture—your life changes but never ends, and it's all about learning, insight and awareness. This is why we compare life to a schoolroom.

We understand your real concern about your son's suffering, both physical and emotional, in the moments before his soul moved on. It is not our role to give you specific details of his last moments. What we can tell you is that at such times of human trauma, the Beloved is present along with the guides of each person. Those whose bodies are dying are held in a great web of love and compassion. To the human observer, all those who died in this violent way may have seemed beyond help, but they were held in the embrace of Love as their bodies could no longer hold their spirits. On that day, as in every death, no one moved on alone without companions to guide the journey toward the Light. Every spirit moves on to explore the next level of its learning. Everyone makes it through to the 'other side.'

Fear and suffering are human experiences, although they don't have to be. They are seen as the illusions they are when spirits are no longer limited by physicality. It is possible to learn the difference between illusion and reality while still on the earth plane. It's possible to learn easily, or you may choose to suffer all the negative emotions. Each of you has the opportunity for the kind of life and death that you need, and choose. The Divine Plan is in place in spite of the evidence of chaos and cruelty on the human plane.

On July 4, 2002, the Committee speaks again to Alison:

As we continue to honor your grief, we declare what the

mind resists—that your son is alive in Spirit; that he is here because he embraced the work that he chose to do on September 11. Now, he is more alive than ever, spreading his enthusiasm and *joie de vivre*. We understand that the loss of his physical presence is painful; and this separation is temporary. You are always reunited with those you love. This truth is not some sentimental piety.

Welles made a soul choice to act in congruence with his highest values. It's not that he chose to 'die.' He remained in the tower to help, making the implicit choice to leave if necessary. The laws of physics were not suspended on September 11.

We bless your journey and remind you that Love is the glue that holds the cosmos in existence. It surely holds the love between you and your beloved son.

THE EXPERIENCE OF WAR

February, 2003, before the start of the Iraqi war:

The struggle in Iraq is for the species' learning. It is an opportunity to witness to the truth, to stand for the evolution of the human spirit. Learning how to live in peace is a task of human evolution. Each person's energy is needed in this time to remind leaders of a larger agenda beyond their myopic vision. Surround them with Love's energy; put aside righteous anger and stand firmly on the side of peace.

This is a time when violence and war can begin to be seen as part of humanity's past. War is a primitive, non-productive way of solving problems. Each of you can embolden yourself to speak *your* truth to the power establishment. Power counts on the disempowerment of the many to maintain the power of the few. But power is all about energy. It is neutral. It can be used for good or for the illusion of evil.

Stand for peaceful solutions in ways that seem right to you. Each person's energy counts toward a critical mass necessary for changing policies from violence to negotiation. You are here to use these skills. Evolution toward the Light is a species-wide effort.

Change happens as Love rules. When fear rules, the results are abuse, fundamentalism, war and violence. As you practice a loving response in every moment, this new way of living becomes doable. That's all that's ever asked of you, and it's an invitation, not a command. And then, of course, you notice how far short of the ideal your behavior is. But you have new opportunities every hour. Do you have the commitment to keep practicing? There is a potent moment when you decide to say a big yes, a grand assent to life on the path of conscious intention. It becomes your north star, your compass.

March, 2003, at the beginning of the Iraqi war:

War is a terrifying teacher, as you are learning. When events of such enormity happen, those who are ready, learn; hearts that have been closed, open and love. This love is the opposite of sentimental emotion. This love persists in spite of hatred, in spite of all reason. This love plugs along, believing in its ultimate power and healing. This love gathers under its wings the frightened, those filled with hubris; it gathers the pro-war and peace factions; it gathers the generals and soldiers, the Iraqis and the Americans. This love is all-encompassing. It has no favorites. It gathers Saddam and Bush equally in its arms. It doesn't have to approve of their behavior. Love by its very nature can only love.

Practicing this non-personal love is a challenge. It's easy to be angry and self-righteous in the midst of so much unconsciousness. But to those of you who are becoming more conscious fall a special challenge: keep your hearts open to love in every small circumstance of your life. Practice faithfully the small easy loves you feel for your family and friends, and for yourself—don't forget yourself! Then when bombs explode and leaders speak propaganda, your habit of loving will help you to open your heart in the presence of the immensity of all that is love's opposite. You are here to learn compassion, and it requires that your heart break open to the unconsciousness of others. Action springs from compassion, and compassion can change your history as a species. Times of war are always pregnant with possibility.

On November 3, 2004, the morning of the American presidential election, the Committee had this to say:

So you think that life cannot go on because your country is on the 'wrong' track? Life is bigger than any one person's or administration's power. Today is another opportunity to remember that Love rules. All the evidence to the contrary is like ashes left after a warming fire. The important thing to remember is your *choice* to light a fire; to be a light bearer during a time you judge as one of darkness and hopelessness.

There have been great periods of darkness on your planet—the Crusades, the Inquisition, the witch burnings, the Holocaust, the ethnic 'cleansings'—all choices made from the dark unconscious side. And it is true that great human suffering followed from these choices.

We remind you, ever so gently, that after today's election has been decided, there is great and holy work to be done. This work cannot be accomplished from a place of hatred or righteous indignation. This new phase of transformation on the planet can happen *only* from a place of love and open-heartedness. Dogmatism, of whatever variety, cries out to be healed of the certainty that it knows all the answers; that it is the vehicle of God's or Allah's will. This view is less than adolescent; it is childish and dangerously naïve.

So what is the 'solution' to these fanaticisms? It is to

make every decision from a place of openhearted love; billions of decisions and acts made from this place. The weight of loving-kindness is necessary to shift the balance on the earth. Each one here now has the opportunity to choose this path. No one is here by accident. No one leaves by accident. The plan of Love remains in place, in a kind of eternal perfection, in the face of all that appears to be the antithesis of Love.

We understand that this process seems imperceptibly, maddeningly slow. Setbacks of consciousness are judged as defeats. And sometimes, those learning to live in the conscious awareness of Love become disheartened. But because Love is the essence of each created being, everyone, no exceptions, is on this plane to *know* rather than simply believe that Love is the true reality. You are ultimately inseparable from the great Love of which we are all a part.

Your work and your play is to manifest love here, now, in every decision, in all your plans, in your memories of the past, in your intentions for the future. All the wars, the inhumanities, the arrogance are ultimately illusion. Because, our dear ones, Love is all there is.

We invite you to choose the reality of Love consciously, in every breath, in every thought, in every interaction. A life lived from this place can literally overcome the dark energy on the earth. We send you light and hope. We challenge you not to become discouraged. Great beings of light are here to help. Call on us. It is our joy to serve.

Why must innocent people suffer as a result of war and greed? How could a loving God allow such tragedies to occur? If we are responsible for our lives and choose the context in which we learn, how could anyone possibly choose such cruel circumstances?

There are no victims. There are only those who choose to be in a particular place at a particular time. We know what we say does not please the mind, but souls sometimes choose extremely difficult outer circumstances in which to learn and grow. And, you may rightly ask, what are babies learning who are dying from starvation and in bombings? We say only that the wisdom and love of their souls has led them to choose this kind of death. There is an inner journey that the baby's soul is taking which is more important than the outer circumstances. Don't be fooled by what appears to be happening. On a soul level, everything is protected and guided. Even though some turnings of the Path seem needlessly difficult, in the midst of the chaos, all is well.

Sometimes the death of an innocent baby happens for some soul lesson that the parents will experience from such a loss. On a soul level, the baby may choose to suffer to uncover the darkness of greed. Or perhaps starvation is a choice of that soul to evoke *your* loving response from across the world. You are not as separate as you might imagine. Every single life affects every other life. It is not an exaggeration to say that you are your brother's and sister's keeper. Every sorrow is your sorrow, and every joy is your joy. What you learn raises the entire pool of consciousness, and your fear holds back the entire show.

While it is true that the darkness of others affects you, it is equally true that your light affects them. When you place yourself on the side of Light, it is not only for your own growth and happiness, but for the collective growth of consciousness toward the Light.

6

Living in the World

Love is all that is Real.

You are not here in this place of duality by chance. This manifestation of your spirit in form was a choice made from the deepest places in your soul. What are the implications of your agreement to make an appearance on earth at this time? When you open your heart to this mystery, you learn that you arrived here with the answers inside of you. You can choose to access your own wisdom or you can ignore and deny it.

In many lifetimes, you've learned well how to do these things. Now it's time to honor your gifts by acknowledging them, and claim your gifts by using them. You have chosen to be here *now* from the beginning of the ages, and we urge you to use the time first for your own highest good and then for the optimum good of all. You have the energy and the resources to realize the potential within you, but the potential needs to become actualized.

REMEMBERING WHO YOU ARE

Remembering is the process of becoming fully human. It is acknowledging the miracle of you, why you are here *now*, what you might contribute to the common good in *this* time, what you might learn and share with others as you open your heart and discover once again who you are.

Of course you *know* who you are, but the contract of the human experience is that you agree to forget for awhile. Then you are given opportunities to remember. Remembering is the glorious process of coming into your own, of reclaiming your power, of saying what you know out loud in the world.

In childhood, many of you were coerced to conform to the values of the adults who held the power in your small world. You were taught not to trust your own feelings. Your needs for play and spontaneity were interrupted by meal times when you weren't hungry and nap times when you weren't sleepy. You were asked to collude in the denial of your own inner knowing. You were rewarded for behavior that often had nothing to do with *your* preferences.

It's not surprising that as adults you don't dare to trust yourselves. As children, many of you learned to pretend to like what you despised and to trust those you distrusted. You were encouraged to say yes when you meant no. Reclaiming your inner knowing has the power to transform your life. You begin to ask—what do I really want to do now, or what is the truth that I need to speak?

You are unique in this time and place. You have agreed to come to the earth plane to learn again what it means to be aware of yourself as this unique person. The remembrance of being is different from doing. Is it possible to remember that you *are* in the midst of a computer glitch? Does remembering who you are while solving a problem change the task, bring meaning to it, change the you that is observing it? We pose these questions not to suggest that you stop for metaphysical thoughts in the midst of installing new software programs, but we remind you that you are no less you in the midst of your distractions.

Follow the promptings of your own deep knowing however they are revealed to you, whether by the wonder of the natural world, the stirring of your heart as you listen to beautiful music, or the synchronous meetings with those who serve as markers on the Path.

Take the time your spirit needs to become acquainted with itself. Your agreement with your soul is to discover who you are beyond circumstance, roles and time. You are here to remember who you are; it's why you show up again and again. As you remember, you become more fully you. Events will change in the outer world as more and more humans learn to remember. It cannot be otherwise. The evolution of consciousness is the result of individual intentions to remember that you are part of Divinity.

How can I remember who I really am in the midst of crisis?

Remember what you already know. And you know a lot—everything you need for the journey. Difficulties arise when you doubt what you know, or when you believe that you can simply think your way through what you perceive as life's big problems.

Problems and crises are a matter of perception. From your soul's perspective, there is nothing to solve, no suffering to be endured. Crises, as the Chinese character says, are opportunities, privileged times when you may choose to come into your heart center. Crises remind you that clever strategies don't always succeed; plans are good to make but they don't always work out; lovers sometimes get bored or scared and leave.

What are you left with when plans fail and lovers leave? How does the love in your heart serve your highest aspirations? Is the reality of Love some New Age fantasy that can leave you as empty as the distorted teaching of God's love preached in many places of worship? You have every right to ask: is this Love at the center of my being real?

We assert that this capital 'L' Love is *all* that is real.

Everything else is transitory, ephemeral. And the fact that you may ask such a provocative question points to your remembering. You ask the questions whose answers you already know. Your spirit says, "Beyond this costume of a body, beyond the façade of time and space, I know." You get a glimpse, you begin to remember, you feel the reality of this Love in your bones, and then a small annoyance or a heartbreak happens and you forget.

This is the game humans agree to play. Then, there comes a time when you realize you're tired of playing the game. Make the decision to consciously remember who you are—hundreds, thousands of times, until your personality is convinced. Then you can *choose* to come into your heart—you will have trained your spirit to be there—and the knee-jerk reactions into judgment and fear will be fewer and fewer. You are in charge of the process. There is no hurry, but in another real sense, it's time, high time. Spirit surrounds you on this journey. You are never alone as you remember that you live in the heart of Love.

BECOMING FULLY HUMAN

(This section includes a potpourri of topics that the Committee has spoken about from time to time; some briefly and others at some length. They are in no particular order.)

GRATITUDE

Gratitude opens a space for you to celebrate your life. Then you remember that you are an expression of Divinity. If you make a habit of celebrating life, you'll perceive your glass half full in the difficult times. Gratitude is the surest way to cause the glass to overflow with the riches that Spirit is eager to bestow upon you. When you are aware of your blessings, your heart is open to make choices of wisdom and compassion.

If you take gifts and blessings for granted, your heart remains unaware of the Giver, and gifts are often not only unacknowledged but unnoticed. Life may then seem stingy and hardscrabble. But when you accept whatever life offers with gratitude, your understanding of what is true and good undergoes a transformation. You train your consciousness to say yes to life. A grateful heart is a powerful force. When you thank Creation for its gifts, it heaps its bounty upon you.

Gratitude enables the Universe to open for you, but this gratitude must be genuine. The process can't work if gratitude is forced or if you are afraid to trust that blessings will show up in your life.

You've chosen to incarnate to learn first to recognize and then accept all that Creation intends for you. It's a joy to fully take in what has already appeared, but giving thanks for what is not yet here requires trust. The more you claim blessings that haven't yet manifested in your life, the more they can appear.

TRUST

It is easy to trust when the Path seems clear, when the sun lights the way. Then, you set out confidently. When the Path is veiled in mist, when clouds cover the sun, when the moon is hidden—then faith lights the way, and trust in the goodness of Creation becomes your compass.

You are here to learn about trust. Opportunities for

practicing trust will keep appearing—the Universe is generous!—until you learn this elemental lesson. It is elemental because it is the *sine qua non*, the 'that without which' your spiritual development becomes sidetracked. Trust must come first, in the thick of darkness, in the murkiness and confusion of not knowing. You agree not to know as the very condition of *beginning* to know and understand.

Trust requires that you do your best: that you plan, organize, figure things out as well as you can, listen to advice, seek expert opinion—and then, let go of the outcome. This isn't naïveté, it is full cooperation with the creativity of the Universe.

Trust is allied with wisdom, which is qualitatively different from knowledge. Nurturing an environment in which your wisdom supports your trust is the mark of a Master. And you are all called to be Masters. This is both your heritage and your ultimate destiny—not scared little souls relieved to be saved and in 'heaven'; rather, Masters who co-create with Spirit. The practice of trust is a beginning step on the Path to full consciousness, to remembering at last who you are.

FAITH

Faith is the impulse to plow beyond the reasonable, beyond the evidence of the senses. It goes beyond the intellect's demands. When you practice faith, you make a decision to believe in the unseen, the immanent. Although the intellect is to be honored as a valuable guide, faith requires a leap to the intuitive. It keeps going against all reasonable expectations, practicing consistency in the midst of the world's capriciousness.

So how can you put faith to work to make your life more successful? First, faith requires a radical decision to believe that you are here by design (both an unimaginably complex and an elegantly simple design) to reveal yourself as a discrete expression of Spirit in time. You are here, temporarily—in this dimension and incarnation—to remember, and forget, as many times as it takes, that you are Spirit embodied and ensouled, and to do the 'work' that this faith implies, indeed requires.

No one forces, no one hustles you along on this journey,

but the imperative is imbedded in your spirit. How long can you resist the call to uncover your true nature, to be God-in-a-body for others to see and love and be moved by? Faith chooses to believe what your mind cannot begin to fathom—that you are here to model Spirit's love, first for yourself and then for others. If you don't believe you're loved (and you can't always *feel* it), you can't love others.

We invite you to hold your unbelief and your doubts tenderly. Faith is a practice, a process, a winnowing of all the doubts. Doubting the reality of this Love of all loves makes perfect intellectual sense. So the challenge is to go beyond human sense to this meta-perspective. We understand that this is harder for those who live lives focused in the mind, but mind can be your ally and companion on the journey. Your intellect will protect you from easy solutions; it will keep you sharp, while reminding you of its limitations.

Faith isn't necessary when life is going well. Faith born of courage digs in its heels and perseveres; it surrenders to what is, exactly as it is. This is the faith that can move mountains. It is the still place in the center of a storm.

Faith is different from the beliefs that religions teach. Faith steps out into the unknown without a map made by others. It chooses to believe in the power and reality of the un-manifest, the yet to be seen and heard. Faith believes that the Divine is working in your life at all times. The cloudy becomes clear when you have faith that you are held in eternal safety, especially when there is no outward evidence for this.

Appreciate the small gifts, the good things that appear in your life, especially in times of trouble. The puzzle pieces of your life will one day fit together and reveal themselves. When you're in the middle of the puzzle, the scattered pieces seem chaotic. Believing that the picture will ultimately make sense helps the puzzle to get solved. The illusion of linear time in which you live makes faith challenging, but it is only the lack of a larger perspective that makes faith necessary at all.

GRACE

Grace is poise, insight, the ease with which you sail through mighty difficulties. It is a gift—unasked for, unsought. Sometimes, you feel grace's presence—you *experience* the love and guidance of the Oneness. More often it's at work anonymously, and you forget that you are held in this divine caring. Grace is the context in which you are guided and protected toward your deepest knowing. It is confirmation of Spirit's presence. It's neither a reward for good deeds nor a spiritual perk that you imagine you can merit by gritting your teeth and avoiding evil. Rather, grace is a way Spirit shows its generosity.

VULNERABILITY

Vulnerability is pure being, without defense, strategy or judgment. It invites you to be open to the heart of the moment while establishing boundaries that honor yourself and others. It doesn't give another permission to manipulate you. Remember, you always collude in manipulation.

Sometimes humans get vulnerability confused with victimization. But there are important differences between being willing to be vulnerable and agreeing to be a victim. Victims are at the mercy of life. They expect the worst, usually get what they imagine and fear, and then bemoan their fate as inevitable. When you are vulnerable, you stand open-hearted, protected in the Light, trusting that your deep wisdom is informed by your higher self.

FORGIVENESS

How do you let go of an old hurt that you've kept close to the heart? Reminding yourself of harsh words exchanged is like refusing to remove a thorn from your finger. If it stays, it festers and consumes your attention. The solution to a thorn is easy—acknowledge the pain, and remove its source. There may be some residual tenderness—perhaps a little scar as a reminder to be careful in the rose garden, but the cause of the pain is gone.

Reluctance to forgive, holding on to an old misunderstanding, causes ongoing pain. Sometimes the pain is acute, and sometimes you've carried it around for so long you hardly notice it. The temporary pain necessary to remove hurts and old anger is worth it. But first you must be willing to acknowledge the discomfort. Forgiveness and letting go of righteousness can become new habits, replacing the old one of holding on to resentment.

Forgiveness begins with you. First, forgive yourself for not being perfect—for hurting, for forgetting, for causing pain. You are exactly where you are supposed to be. So, really, there is nothing to forgive.

Forgiving others is an act of will. Make no mistake, you forgive others for *you*, not for them. This isn't narcissism—it's basic pragmatism. If you don't forgive those who've wronged you, *you* carry with you the weight of the injury. When you forgive those who have hurt you, you release their hold over you.

Feelings are habits, and take a while to catch up with intention. When the habitual hurt comes up, release it, surround it with light and gently send it on its way. The space that forgiveness opens will fill with peace and opportunities for new learning.

THE WILL

One kind of will lives in your head and pushes to get its own way. Another kind comes from the heart and is informed by your connection to Higher Intelligence. *This* will is humble; it doesn't have to have everything figured out.

How do you move from an intellect-centered, self-centered will to one that is connected to the heart? Allow the wisdom and love in your heart to guide your head. Love is never a waste of time; it can never lead you astray. *Willing* to be in your heart breaks through the illusion of time, and creates space in your life for the agenda of your spirit. A retraining of the will is a longer process. It's like taking vows. You assent in a formal, ritualistic way, and then practice living out these promises day by day.

The will is at its most effective when it partners with a heart open to Love and its leadings. Then it cuts through the brambles of self insisting on *its* way. This awareness opens doors, offers insights, and clears the Path as you walk out onto it. It enables mind and heart to work together.

PRAYER

Prayer is not about asking to fix anything, because nothing needs fixing. You don't have to urge a reluctant God to solve the problems in your life or in the world. All the negativity that you see in the world is a kind of necessary purging. Hold in the Light what you don't understand. This is the only kind of prayer needed.

Many of you were taught as children that prayer was a dutiful ritual that you *should* perform. Some of the old styles of praying are ways to perpetuate control and fear: seeking pardon for your sins, begging to be saved from a fate worse than death, pleading for help against temptation, asking for protection from your human nature.

When you pray, you may or may not use words. It's less about words and more like an expectant kind of listening. Prayer as listening has been available to humans since their earliest development. In Western cultures, this way of praying is difficult because Western mind has been trained to talk to itself incessantly. Early humans better intuited their potential for connecting with the Divine, and the connection they had within themselves to Spirit.

In this era, so-called primitive peoples still express their spirituality in ways that may seem like superstition to an educated mind. But don't be too quick to judge. The minds of these humans aren't filled with the clutter that interferes with easy access to their spirits.

We're not suggesting that prayer can never be formulated with words. Creatures who naturally use words also use them to communicate with Spirit. But be aware that this kind of praying can become a monologue. The essence of prayer is communication, and this requires reciprocity, a mutual exchange. This is where listening comes in. Petitioning, worrying out loud is just the beginning of prayer. The second and more fruitful part is a willingness to be open to what comes into the silent space created by your listening. Making this space in an intentional way invites the participation of Spirit, who is also a part of you. Then you choose to be in the presence of Love, this presence that sustains you in existence.

You are on the cusp of accessing new ways to Spirit, of experiencing the inner wisdom and love that is your birthright. The way in is through the door of silence—the commodity that appears to be in such short supply in most lives. Yet, it is possible to find that silent place in your soul that allows your spirit's wisdom to be uncovered.

The process takes practice, patience, persistence and a

willingness to let go of the struggle. It reminds us of that aphorism, 'Let go and let God.' Really, nothing is required of you except that you show up. The way in to the center of the soul costs nothing, requires no degrees or equipment. It is available to all.

This inward journey both calls for and results in a change of consciousness—a conversion, to borrow a religious term. Though the religions of the world have mostly strayed far from the wisdom and insights of their founders, the truth in them can be found in their traditions of contemplation and meditation.

It's never too late to start on this Path. Although setting aside time for quiet listening is important, a habit of inner listening can permeate the entirety of your days. Your eternal core is there to access in the midst of necessary tasks and busyness. When you cultivate a quality of quiet expectation and listening, you discover not chaos or an empty shell at your center, but the Love that is your essence. You experience a sharing in that cosmic Love that many call by names such as Yahweh, Buddha, Jesus, Krishna—all ensoulments of Love.

INTUITION

Intuition is the way the Creator guides you along the way. It is the silent prompting of Divine inspiration, a collaboration with your deepest knowing. Intuition is not linear. It makes use of hunches, serendipity, coincidence.

Learning to trust your intuition can change your life in a powerful way. Intuition bypasses the stage of figuring things out—it goes straight to the heart of desire; it leaps over the fences of organization. And sometimes it makes mistakes, or at least appears to. True intuition never makes mistakes, although following its promptings can sometimes seem foolhardy. It's a skill to be developed, and you can improve it by using and testing it out.

Experiment with going inside for guidance, even when making small decisions, as training for your intuition. It's similar to learning to speak a new language or play a musical instrument. In the beginning, you feel clumsy, but soon, what was so difficult becomes automatic. You stop thinking about every word or where to place your fingers.

You may wonder how safe it is to trust intuition. Often it seems to fly in the face of logic. How can you distinguish between what is coming from your impulses and needs and what is coming from your spirit? Fear of following intuition comes from a place in you that is afraid to make a mistake. Mistakes are as important to the Path as accomplishments. Everything experienced on the Path is there for your learning.

Control over outer events is one of the favorite illusions of the earth plane. The good news is that there's a reward for letting go of control. When you get beyond the fear that life will be out of control, it begins to flow creatively, and you can more fully use your intuition. Then, intuition becomes the faithful servant of your mind, not some quirky impulse to be ignored or mistrusted. As you practice trusting your intuition, even as it goes against logic, illusions begin to fall away in front of your eyes. A life lived from this place becomes simple and luminous.

It is possible, however, to fine-tune your intuition. When an inspiration tugs at your consciousness, check in with your body. Does this action or idea feel comfortable in the belly, in your heart space? Your body is not only the vehicle that carries you around in the world, it's also a repository of ancient wisdom.

Next, examine your feelings. How does this intuition make you feel deep down—centered and energetic, or scattered and edgy? Then check with the mind for its feedback. Is this impulse loving, realistic, in harmony with your highest goals? If all this exploration leaves you with a sense of peace, then the intuition is probably valid. If there is a sense of *should* in what you think you intuit, this is the voice of fear and old conditioning. What makes you truly happy is exactly what you ought to be doing.

After this preparation, test out your intuition in the world. If it was a valid one, remember what you learned for the next opportunity. You *can* learn to trust your deep wisdom in a child-like way and act on your intuition with confidence. The more you practice, the better you get at it, and the more the world, persons and events become vehicles for the revelation of your intuition.

TRUTH

Truth is a continuum, an ever-changing revelation, expanding as the holder of the truth is able to contain it. Truth expands and changes as a person is able to perceive the larger picture. It's not that a former belief was wrong; it's more that it no longer serves the purpose of the soul's evolving consciousness. A child outgrows his clothes—the clothes weren't 'in error.' The problem with dogma in the old model of truth is that it allows no room for discovery, either in science or spirituality.

Truth is dynamic, not static. What you believed yesterday you may need to adjust in the light of others' discoveries and your new experience and insights. A law of nature may not remain 'true' forever. Does this model mean that nothing is ultimately true? No, rather it means that *everything* is contained in the process of new discovery on the physical level and in soul growth on the spiritual level. This is cause for rejoicing, not despair, because every consciousness and concept is moving toward the full experience of the One.

The Earth as Home

The earth is always teaching if you are receptive to learning from her. During the heart of winter when all nature sleeps and dreams, allow yourself this dream time as well. Are human beings wiser than the creatures that sleep through this season? The birds accept the food set out for them. They don't build nests or nurture their young during the cold. They survive because of the gifts offered by the earth.

Use the gift of snow's silence to go deep into the wisdom of your soul. If you take the time for this, the bumpy road will smooth out, and the space and simplicity that you seek will allow your life to flourish and blossom, even in the midst of winter.

In the season of high spring, when the earth explodes with beauty, shouting praise in the rushing streams, singing love songs in the voices of spring peepers, can you doubt for a moment that the earth is held in Love? The perfection of the unfolding of each species of flower, plant and tree, the birth of each animal and insect is a reminder of Love. The hummingbird hovering at the window is a confirmation of the perfection of creation. The blossoms that fill the air with fragrance and fall to the ground are a sign that what is beautiful is not lost. Is an apple less beautiful than the flower that was its beginning? Is a wrinkled face less lovely than a baby's smile? Is a dandelion less than a rose?

Can you feel the earth's breath, the pulse of its being, as you walk through the woods on a May morning? Humans are becoming conscious of the earth as a living being. If a trillium blooming unnoticed in the woods is alive, can the earth that supports it be any less alive?

Humans' growing awareness of their responsibility for the health of the planet is a collaboration of love to which the earth can respond. This is a time in history when an evolutionary leap is possible both for the earth and her peoples. These two interdependent strands of evolution influence each other. Honor the planet; appreciate her protection, beauty and endless creativity. Out of this attitude of respect will come individual and collective right action.

Be heartened by the individual changes that are allowing the earth to begin to heal from centuries of neglect and exploitation. Intentional loving choices that you make every day are the way this healing happens. Become models to your children as you teach them new ways to protect the planet.

Humankind is challenged these days, not by an angry Old Testament God, but by the forces of nature. The planet has evolved over eons and some humans now live in dangerous places. Know that your spirit is protected even when you make a choice to live in a risky physical place. Everyone is here to flower—to realize themselves, and some breakthroughs can happen even in the midst of human chaos. But chaos and disaster always remain peripheral to your eternal safety.

You might wonder—does Love, the creative force of the cosmos, cherish a rich man more than one who lives in poverty? It would seem that Love has favorites, but this is another of earth's illusions. Does Love discriminate against the poor who lose what little they possess in hurricanes and earthquakes? While it may be tempting to become disheartened and believe this, know that it's impossible for Love to act against its nature.

This is a time of great potential healing for many.

Healing energy is surrounding Earth in a way it hasn't for eons. The energy is particularly strong in certain locations, and people are often inexplicably drawn to these places. Many are discovering them and sharing this information. It isn't necessary to live in such high-energy locations, but it can be helpful at certain stages of your growth. The collective intention of like-minded persons living close together is a support, whether or not you know them personally.

If you need to live in a powerful place, you'll be drawn to one. You can also ask to be in such places in spirit. This is good practice for being there in your body. Ask to be in a place that supports your highest evolution, and be prepared for surprises.

Recently, there has been a proliferation of information about crop circles. This renewed interest reminds us of one of our favorite themes: that humanity is poised for an evolutionary leap. It will be accomplished with great help from high beings who are teaching truths that you have intuited since your beginnings. You are not alone in the

Universe, and there is an elegant plan for the evolution of consciousness in all creation.

The circle makers are passionately dedicated to giving you glimpses of physical and spiritual reality and their links with all of creation. Crop circles are examples of the on-going creativity and subtlety of Love in action. Like sand paintings, they are short-lived, but contain within them ways of unlocking secrets of the universe.

Crop formations that are appearing in many parts of the world demonstrate that Spirit is in charge of the plan of evolution. This is a way the All That Is demonstrates its presence and love. Crop circles are a way to open hearts, to give you new reasons to remember who you are, where you've come from and your place in the ongoing yet ever-changing web of Love at the heart of creation. Think of them as love letters to all created beings from their Creator.

After the tsunami on December 26, 2004:

The laws of your world, which have evolved over eons, work in predictable ways and produce outcomes on the physical plane. Events sometimes happen which set in motion great changes, viewed by humans as catastrophes. And they *are*, from the perspective of the personalities affected by these sudden changes.

When viewed from a larger perspective, physical disasters evoke a great outpouring of love to welcome all the souls who find themselves so unexpectedly in spirit; to care for the children and for those who are confused or fearful. There are special guides who volunteer for this work of love and do it with great tenderness.

For those not affected, the task is to open your hearts, to have compassion for those who must cope with so many losses. The human community has an opportunity to put aside differences—to work for reconstruction, to donate money, to adopt children, above all to hold in the Light all those affected. It's an unprecedented opportunity to send love to that part of the planet. If you doubt how opening your hearts can help those who are suffering, we assure you, it helps both those who receive and those who give.

Souls agree to come to the earth plane for many different reasons. We may stretch your belief system by saying that each person who 'died' in the tsunami chose this on a soul level. We know your personalities resist believing this. But we also say, respectfully, that your beliefs do not have the power to affect reality.

You have an opportunity to wrap your spirit around this human calamity, to hold it in Light and Love. Earth is a place of learning, and this is a time for great acceleration in the pace of that learning. It is a privilege to be in a body in a time of such great potential.

EMBRACING CHANGE

By their very nature, created beings change. When you are in the flow of creation it's safe to embrace change. Resistance, fear, clinging—all are useless strategies in the vastness of the energy that is the life force. When you *choose* the process of change, you more easily release your preferences. You accept what is with trust and curiosity, with a laying aside of your own agenda.

We suggest that you actively and consciously collaborate with the energy of creation. Then you can fulfill your purpose here no matter how circumstances change, because you are choosing to be an active participant in creation.

When you accept change as your ally, life unfolds in surprising ways. You no longer have to hold on tight to remain safe, because you *are* safe, eternally.

Without change, there could be no growth or renewal. Protection is always with you during times when change equals major life transition or loss. Sometimes, losses are necessary to make way for the new. Asking for protection and acknowledging it, raises your awareness of the help that is present. There is nothing to fear in the process.

Think of times of transition as ones of weeding your spiritual garden. Weed out things in your life that inhibit healthy growth—persons and situations that stand in the way of the Light. It is well within your power to remove hindrances from your life. Be guided by the promptings that come from your inner sources of wisdom.

This is a time of great change—for you, for your beloveds, for everyone on the planet. Change is always accompanied by discomfort. It requires you to go beyond the everyday, the commonplace; to venture forth to new places in your life and spirit. The time for planning change, thinking about it, envisioning it, is past. Adventure is now for everyone—because *everyone* on earth is here to go beyond old boundaries. Familiar patterns may be very comfortable or very painful. You are being asked to let go of both your comfort and your pain. It may well be that giving up your pain is more challenging than giving up your comfort. In any case, it's time for new challenges, time to begin living this new model of reality.

How this change will look in your life is unique to each of you. The challenge is to observe what the needed change is, where and with whom, and to what purpose. After noticing comes the commitment to make the change in each interaction, in your motivation and intention. Each internalized change leads to the next. But first must come the awareness of the need for change. This is the way that world change, species change, happens.

Sentient beings know at some level that great changes are afoot on the planet and in human evolution. These changes are confirmation that Spirit is palpably at work in the world—on the earth itself and in all earth's creatures.

We say these things to offer you hope, not to initiate fear. The disguises of hatred, warmongering, homophobia, racism, gender bias and classism have been believed in for long periods of your evolution. Now you are ready to take off these costumes and reveal yourselves as incarnations of the Love from which all creation arises.

The long history of UFO sightings, crop circles, energy workers, healers and channelers is helping to break through the old intellectual paradigm. That model was useful, but now it needs to be expanded to include human beings who are co-creators in this new order in which humanity begins to see beyond the borders of countries and cultures. This new paradigm expands your vision so that you experience the connectedness of humans to each other, and the primacy of Love in all creation. This is why you're here, why you've chosen to come in at this time.

7

Acting in the World

*You are here to do what
can be done only by an embodied spirit.
It is a challenging assignment, not for the timid.*

R ight action in your life and in your sphere of influence follows from receptivity to the inner world of Spirit. It's a consequence of consciously choosing to be in Spirit's presence. A Spirit-filled and informed life is both inner and outer directed. The inner growth is never without some outer manifestation.

Without you, the God of whom you speak so often in exalted terms would be less than whole. Can you begin to understand how essential you are? You have the opportunity to accomplish your unique tasks and to live your authentic life. Although the word 'tasks' has an aura of struggle about it, your authentic work is synonymous with joy and effortless creation. Ease in fulfilling your role in the world may be the most difficult quality to accept. Remember that struggle is always a sign that you're stumbling on the Path.

Who are you in your essence? Who are you in the world? Does your presence inspire others? What is your purpose here, in this time, in this body, personality and gender? What is the contribution you can make? What have you already done, and what is left to do?

Your intention to make peace is as important as a leader's intention to make war. But you say—he has the power, and I don't. Don't be so sure! You will never experience your power if you don't use it. The challenge is to take part in peacemaking in ways that empower you and others. Your consciousness *does* matter, and your personal soul work, your own turning toward the Light, is a prerequisite for effective peace work in the world.

If your actions come from love, don't try to calculate the outcomes. Don't keep track of the impact *your* contribution has made. If you watch in this way, it will seem that your efforts don't count, and you'll turn away in discouragement. When a common energy is focused on good, events can and do change. The pool of consciousness is critical in any global change and you are an essential part of that pool.

REMEMBERING WHY YOU ARE HERE

You are here for good reasons—soul reasons, heart reasons. We remind you of what you know and forget and remember again—the challenge of taking human form, an assignment not for the timid. You are more than a human, although you are here to do what can be done only by an embodied spirit.

Everyone is here to do the work of Spirit in a body—including the man with rotting teeth whose way crosses yours at the checkout counter, and the daughter of a cherished friend who lives with profound disabilities. It is your challenge to see their spirits past the veil of your limitations. It is your challenge to practice humility here, to ignore the temptation to feel superior. They may well be your teachers, as you are all each others' teachers and students in turn. No one comes into your life by accident. We understand it's difficult to believe this, because life often seems full of random encounters.

You are in the process of stripping away all that prevents your essence from growing and expressing itself. Although you become most fully yourself for your own sake, you are also here to light the way for each other. You participate in a counterpoint of solitude and community, both sounding your own themes and weaving melodies together with others. And you learn to use discernment about which themes to play and which to discard.

Everyone is here purposefully—no exceptions. Try not to judge the unconsciousness in the world. Judgment drags everyone down. Evolution is a slow and messy process. Your business is your evolution toward Love. This is the most you can do, both for yourself and others. The plan of Love is in place. It always has been. The earth school is one of intense learning, but not one to be feared. Nothing can ever harm your essence. All pieces of this great mosaic are designed to fit together perfectly because Spirit is perfection, and you are all discrete pieces of that perfection. Remember this when you stumble, when you don't trust your Path. The essence of evolution is remembering again and again who you are and why you're here. And some of you are here to help others remember as well.

I am overwhelmed by the enormity of global poverty and hunger, by epidemics that could be easily prevented, and by the rise of religious fundamentalism. What is my responsibility to alleviate this suffering?

Mind wants to understand a problem, then find a way to fix it. We may challenge your belief system by suggesting that everyone is where he/she has agreed to be. Incarnation is an agreement with Love. Emaciated bodies, all the uncounted thousands orphaned and those dying of malaria and HIV/AIDS are calling out for your compassion and for your non-personal love—loving them simply because they are humans like you, with hopes and dreams and fears for the future.

What good will loving them do? Will it assuage their suffering or their grief? No love sent forth ever goes astray or is wasted, and compassion precedes action. This isn't a sentimental gesture; it is a response of spirit to spirit. No person can feed all the hungry, but their hunger may evoke a response in you. It's a balance—doing what your intuition and means suggest, while still remaining light-hearted. Your anxiety will not feed the hungry, nor will your anger or guilt.

Some of you may decide to do concrete things such as volunteering to feed the hungry in your community, or visiting the sick and lonely. Or your response may be to continue doing what you do in the world as well as you can.

Religious fundamentalists who ignore the environment because they believe the Rapture is immanent are learning about fantasy on the way to reality. Those who believe that wars are punishments meted out by an angry God delay efforts at peacemaking. Zealots are learning all about zealotry on their journeys to Love. We understand that these journeys seem misguided, off the Path, but no journey is wasted or irrelevant. Side-trips are necessary on many journeys home. Everyone will get there, and the timing for each is perfect. All the winding journeys back to Love take each soul where it needs to go.

It is not for anyone to judge another's journey. The plan is in place in the face of all the evidence to the contrary. Each discrete part of Love, each conscious spirit returns, ultimately, to Love.

CLAIMING YOUR POWER

The intention to claim your power is the beginning of its appearance in your life. When you claim your power, life changes at its core. This emerging power opens new doors and closes others. It allows the Path to show itself clearly. If you're not quite willing to believe this, be gentle with your-self—the part of you that holds back, fearing the power inherent in your gifts. At times this part has served you well, but now it's time for you to not only claim your power but to live it. It is safe to do this, *and* it requires courage. Claiming your unique gifts of Spirit requires a willingness to step into the unknown and trust life's purposes for you. It means surrendering the will of the personality that wants what it wants when it wants it.

Accepting your gifts is exactly that—opening your arms wide to receive them, while putting aside your fear of opening your heart to the love of the Giver. You are never in danger in the presence of Love. Trust this life-giving, life-supporting Love even if you can't always trust yourself. The paradox is that the more you trust the part of you that is Love, the more you can trust and love all of your parts, even those with the bruises and scars of the past.

Your unique gifts are the manifestations of the power you claim. It's useful to prepare for them by clearing away all that clutters your life. Impulses to organize and simplify are good ones, for the clearer your life becomes, the more room there is for collaboration with Spirit.

Beyond accepting your gifts, hold them lightly and playfully. The light-hearted collaborators with Spirit are the ones who get the most done, and with the least effort. Claiming your power is a new way to function in the world. It's neither logical nor linear; it requires only an open heart, and a willingness to learn and accept what is offered.

CLAIMING ABUNDANCE

The way to abundance is to first accept its reality in your life. Abundance is your rightful heritage. It happens naturally when you recognize that you co-create your experience with Spirit. Begin by claiming what you already possess—talents, loves, emotions, possessions—then use these gifts for the good of yourself and others. The Universe isn't limited. Rather, you limit yourself by your belief in limitation. Belief in lack is what keeps the flow of abundance in check.

It's important to fully appreciate what is already present, because what *is* here helps you to trust the not-yet-manifest. Turn toward what is not yet here as if it were already appearing in whatever ways you desire, and give thanks for it. The more you claim unseen blessings, the more easily they can appear. Being in the stream of abundance is bound to create surprises. Creation is eager, even impatient, to cooperate with you. You have everything you need for this journey, *and*, there will be further manifestation in the world when your spirit is ready. If you acknowledge the riches that you have, and claim your birthright as part of Divinity, gifts will not only appear, they may threaten to overwhelm you.

True abundance begins in your spirit, and moves toward physical manifestation. It isn't dependent on the world's rules. Practice using your intuition and trust that your needs will be met. You still have to do your part, but struggle can be replaced by an awareness that you're 'in the flow.' It takes courage to live this way, because old conditioning is so pervasive.

Those of you on a conscious spiritual path are often confused about financial abundance. Money isn't the root of all evil. It's a useful and necessary commodity. Unless you're a monk or a nun supported by a community, you need it. Unless you grow your own food and weave your own cloth, you need it. Wampum or stock certificates, it's a medium of exchange.

Money becomes an ally when you welcome it and are open to receiving what you need. If you think of money as filthy lucre, you unconsciously protect yourself from it. If you fear money's lack, you say, vibrationally, "Keep away from me!" and it obliges.

Letting go of worry about money is a choice. What a wonderful practice, to give up the habit of worry. This includes talking about lack and fear. Watch lovingly what comes out of your mouth. It's like learning a new language to go with a new way of living.

Look at your history—have you died of starvation or had only pine needles to cushion your tired head? Even if you were to starve to death, as many do, your spirit would still be perfectly safe. You can't fall out of life. Your life may change form, but safety is a given.

Are you willing to give up the money struggle? Saying yes once isn't enough, when the habit of struggle is so ingrained. Let go of the tension that anxiety produces, and forge a new habit of consciousness that allows you to find right livelihood and enough money to live comfortably.

This new habit accepts the abundance that surrounds you and the gifts offered, *especially* when they're not yet manifest. Releasing struggle reveals a new way to live. If this sounds simplistic or magical, we say only that it's a natural law of creation. Trust builds a bridge to manifestation; it empowers you to accept the abundance that waits eagerly for you.

Following your heart as a path to freedom and abundance may seem an impractical way to meet your financial obligations, but Spirit's ways are not the ways of the world. Begin and continue doing what you love to do, and release the rest. It *is* safe to live this way.

Money is energy. Let go of the belief that it's impossible to be paid for doing what you love and what you do best. Your loves are the precise markers of abundance. Follow your passion and people will pursue you with money in their hands. It's perfectly legitimate to accept payment for doing what you love. Accepting money for doing what you hate or what you do out of fear comes close to exploiting your employer and behaving unethically. Not settling for security is where faith comes in. Saying no to cleaning other people's toilets can be an act of self-love, unless you do such a job out of conscious loving choice.

However, don't feel you're abandoning the Path if you must do something temporarily to sustain your human needs. Sometimes abundance comes in the form of a job that doesn't fulfill your heart's desire. When you accept such work with a light heart, not with a sense of burden, you're able to move on more easily. Welcome money as a friend and a facilitator. Thank it for being in your life, and it will remain there and grow fat for you.

How can I trust, in the midst of financial uncertainty, that abundance will come?

When you remember how, until now, you have had your needs met, it becomes easier to trust the generosity of the Universe that such abundance will continue. We don't suggest that you deny your concerns. Instead, hold them in the context of the Love that both transcends you and *is* you. Right action always follows from awareness and trust in the power of Love.

You may think this is strange advice when you're worrying about how to support yourself and your family. But we are not unrealistic dreamers. First things first. Love— first for yourself, then for others. The way will unfold as you step out. And if you don't believe us, that's all right too, but step out anyway. There is special grace in stepping out into the darkness, persevering in the midst of doubt and unknowing. Your steps are guided no less in the dark.

Trust in the integrity and wisdom of the creative intelligence in which you participate. You are not merely acted upon, you are an actor in your human drama. You can change the script when it doesn't suit you. You have this power, but living this way requires boldness and creativity.

A conscious, willed alignment with Love can create miracles that circumvent the usual earthly rules. Spirit loves single-mindedness and clarity of intention. These qualities help get your work done efficiently. Struggle is about trying to do it yourself, by your own effort and vigilance. Such hard work is no longer necessary when you're in the stream of Light. Your path becomes clear when you remember that you are a partner in the creation of your life.

Why do greedy people sometimes have great abundance?

Unconscious abundance is like starving at a banquet. Greed doesn't trust the generosity of the Giver. No matter how much greedy people seem to be enjoying themselves and their wealth, there is a place in them that is bankrupt.

More than anything, they fear that their abundance will disappear.

Don't fret if the outcome of greed appears to be abundance. Unconscious wealth isn't real. It's one of earth's illusions. Some are here to learn the lessons inherent in this kind of illusion. It's not for anyone to judge or envy the path of another.

THE SCHOOL OF LONGING

Your longings are the spiritual children yet to be born to you. Hold them in your heart. They are powerful signs that point you toward the agenda of your spirit. Longings illumine the Path and guide you toward remembering.

There is, in each of you, a deep yearning that shows itself on many levels. Sometimes it masquerades as greed, ostentatious consumption or promiscuity—more expensive cars, more sex, all in an attempt to fill a gnawing emptiness. Some feel it's safer to skim life's pleasures than to drink deeply and quench the thirst of an ever-present desire.

It's okay to satisfy some superficial desires, because without a taste of satisfaction, it's hard to stay the course and explore what's deeper. Eventually, longing breaks through whatever distractions you invent. This deep longing comes from the essence of your being. It's a gut feeling that says, "Is this all? There must be something more!"

Allow the *energy* in your longings, not necessarily the longings themselves, to be your guide. Yearning, even for trivial things, can serve the soul in this ongoing school of longing. Desire for spiritual gifts isn't entirely separate from desire for a trip around the world. These yearnings are guides to the possible. Place your dreams in the heart of desire, then let go of concern about their fulfillment.

Longing for gifts of Spirit such as love, purpose and creativity, keeps you attuned to intuition and guidance. Satisfying spiritual hungers is a Divine collaboration. When you've done all you can do, take time to be still. Listen to the guidance within the wellsprings of desire. All desire is in your heart to guide you to the Divine spark at your center. Longings are road signs on the soul's way home to itself. Hold them tenderly, but let them prod you on as well. They light the way and fuel the fires of intention and creativity. When desires light your Path, they become congruent with the agenda of your Higher Self. Visualizing these desires fulfilled and centering your spirit on such a vision helps to make them manifest.

THE POWER OF INTENTION

Focusing on an intention is inherently neutral. If you focus on negative visions that you fear and worry about, they may come true. This is simply universal law at work. The good news is that the same law works for the realization of your highest dreams. The difference is in resolving to be in the positive stream of this energy of intention. This requires a re-training of old thought habits. Turning aside each negative thought requires an attentive consciousness. Unconsciousness runs the negative tapes over and over and deepens those pathways in the brain. The brain is a tool of consciousness to be trained. It's very much like a computer that spews forth what's fed into it. Intend to replace the 'garbage in, garbage out' syndrome with 'desire in, manifestation out.'

Visualize what you want to do, where you'd like to be and with whom. This practice doesn't have to be part of a long meditation. Whenever you think of it, do it. Then let the results go, and be prepared for surprises. Divine Mind is unlimited and infinitely creative.

It's possible to sabotage yourself by having vague goals. The more specific the desire, the more the Universe collaborates with you to satisfy it. The more clearly you visualize the realization of your fulfilled desire, the easier it is for it to manifest. Try this lightheartedly, as an experiment in working with universal law. Spirit knows your needs before you ask, *and* loves to be asked. Ask for what you need or what you think you need. If your perception is off a bit, no matter. Intention is what's important.

The next step is to acknowledge that what you've asked for is on its way to manifestation. Spirit isn't stingy. It doesn't withhold blessings from its beloveds; its essence is Love and so can act only in congruence with its nature.

As you wait for manifestation in form and time, you have opportunities to practice faith and patience. While you're waiting, prepare your life by simplifying it. Develop a sense of what is right for you to spend time on and what isn't—what teachings have a ring of truth, to be further explored, and which are peripheral, not necessarily wrong, but peripheral to *your* path and purpose.

8

Loving in the World

The criterion is always—what would Love do?

It was on an afternoon in early November, when my boys were toddlers, that I was visited by my beloved friend Bob, who had died in a plane crash several years earlier. It was an ordinary afternoon except for the fragrance of roses that filled the living room. The boys wanted to watch their favorite preschool program. As I turned on the TV, I was surrounded by an overwhelming presence of love that I knew somehow was coming from Bob. Then I remembered that it was his birthday.

Later, I remembered that he always sent me roses on special oc-
casions. (Catholics have a belief that when a saint is present, the
fragrance of roses is in the air. They call it the 'odor of sanc-
tity.')

Your calling and your heritage is to be the creator in your world—the spirit of love to the alienated, the spirit of compassion to those who suffer, the spirit of wisdom to the ignorant. Love needs you to be a messenger of its power on the earth. Without you, Love's power is diminished. Every coming to life in a body is always an agreement with Love—to make Love real and believable in the world through you. Each incarnated soul is an essential part of this tapestry of Love-made-real. Everyone has a unique piece to contribute to the whole: everyone—no exceptions.

The good news is that life on your planet is lived in the context of Love. We know that this concept goes against the commonly held wisdom, because many of your experiences seem to be love's opposite. But all the negativity that surrounds life—the pettiness, the lust for power, the cruelty—cannot diminish the power of love.

Humans practice love imperfectly, but it's important to practice. It's the small daily decisions to act from a loving place that make a powerful difference to the whole of humankind. These decisions can lessen the force of violence on a global scale. Although it's often upsetting, it's important that you know what's going on in the world. The genocides in Africa affect you because those who are suffering are your brothers and sisters.

A collective intention to counteract hate with love can change the nature of humanity and influence the evolution of the species. The extreme negativity of many current events can serve as a powerful impetus for change, and change happens when there is a critical mass of those who choose to make every decision from a place of love.

This means speaking truth to power; it means taking a stand for love. And sometimes, it requires remaining silent instead of expressing your opinion. The criterion is always—what would love do? Will you sometimes make mistakes coming from this place? Yes—and you're here on the earth plane to learn from so-called mistakes. In the larger context there are no mistakes. Everything is chosen by you for your learning, to elicit your compassion in the presence of suffering, including *your* suffering.

This process of unfolding love may seem slow. Often it is, but there are opportunities for breakthroughs in evolution when the species is ready to learn something new. You are living in one of these times. Again we say—it is a privilege and a challenge to be in a body now.

Universal Mind longs for wholeness on the earth, a global unity that can be realized only by fully conscious humans. Wholeness happens when you focus your life on those things which really matter. You are here to strip away all that distracts you from being 'in Love.' All that you might label the antithesis of love reminds you what love is not, what is love disguised or love resisting itself. The desire to be in Love's presence is what drives the cosmos. Everyone's ultimate purpose is to be where Love is with no distractions or ambivalence, doing whatever Love does.

It's so tempting to believe the evidence of your senses, particularly when that evidence suggests bad news, but acceptance of the reality of Love can transform the deepest human fears. The cosmos would disappear if it were not held in this ever-present Love. We proclaim love in the presence of suffering, loneliness, abandonment, fear, even hatred. Love *is*.

When you take love seriously, life honors your intention and takes *you* seriously, and the outer world more and more reflects the inner. When every decision and action is made from love, what is peripheral falls away, and what is essential for the journey becomes clear.

Of course, you cannot save the world, which is the same as loving it, until you love yourself. When you love yourself, you are free to act from a place of love. If you're afraid of love, or its lack, it's back to the drawing board of your life to try again. Ask that you be 'in love' every moment. You already are, but asking helps you to remember. Then we guarantee your journey will cease to be a struggle and the Path will be illumined as you step forth.

LOVE AS LIFE'S CURRICULUM

To learn the nature of Love is why you're here—to pour

out your love in open-hearted vulnerability, to discover love unexpectedly in yourself, to give it away foolishly, to be a spendthrift in the name of love. Don't hold some back for a rainy day. There are no rainy days in Love's kingdom.

Spirit is Love, and that Love continues to create itself as a necessity of its nature. Creation, in all its numberless manifestations, is the way Spirit makes love to everything; and the purpose of everything is to reflect love back to the Source. You become part of a Möbius strip* of love and creativity as you become *you* most completely.

When you are aware of being one with Love, existence is pure revelation. Love shows its wonder in as many ways as hearts are open to receive it. You need only look and listen. A daffodil is a microcosm that contains within it the splendor and perfection of creation. And creation is a manifestation of Love—there is no other reason for the daffodil's existence. Does this give you an inkling of the love that is present in each act of creation?

Love is the raw material of creation: every thought,

A closed loop with a half-twist in it, that appears to have no beginning or end.

being and object is an expression of Love. Even negative and unforgiving thoughts are part of Love. The ability to think them, the voice to speak them, is Love offering you the opportunity to see what is useful and what is hurtful. Love offers you a choice to change your response, but it doesn't force you to be loving. Love is so patient that it allows you the freedom to be unloving. When you've had enough, you are ready to open your heart to more loving choices.

Nothing is wasted in this creation. All unkindness, greed, cruelty and abuse of power are ultimately experienced in the service of Love. So it's not for anyone to judge others' journeys. They are experiencing exactly what they need on *their* Path. You can't disown the cruel and unconscious ones. You may abhor their actions, but you know in your open-hearted moments that they are companions on the Path. Terrorists, rapists, murderers—they are all part of you; they are your brothers and sisters, your spiritual family. Sometimes, their behavior makes *your* life dangerous or uncomfortable and affects *your* Path. But since you are all part of the One, what is happening to the 'worst' of you is also happening to you. What you experience with others can help your journey or hinder it. In one sense, there *are* no others. You and they are all together in this vast web of Love.

We offer this perspective to encourage both humility and hope. You are all capable of cruel thoughts and deeds, and you are all part of the Light. Your journeys home are entwined in sometimes wonderful, sometimes challenging, but always mysterious ways. It cannot be otherwise, since each of you is a discrete part of Love.

The will and the love of the Highest is manifest even in circumstances that seem at odds with such manifestation. Such is the slow and certain path of Love in your world. We don't measure progress or 'success' as you do. Spirit's time is expansive. It cannot be squeezed into your model of linear time. We remind you that your path is guided toward perfection in the midst of imperfection—yours and everyone's. All apparent evidence to the contrary is as evanescent as dust motes in a ray of sunlight.

You see, the emergence of Love's reality cannot be

hidden or defeated or ultimately ignored by any earth events. Evolution may appear circuitous, but it's spiraling always toward more light. So all is well, our beloveds. All is well in the thick of hatred and violence. The momentum toward the good of all cannot be thwarted. It can be circumvented, ignored, disguised as evil, but never defeated. Love *is* the reality of the created Universes. Love is the very material of creation. Remember—love's opposites always point toward Love, this Love that is present even in the midst of war and hubris. The more love is denied, the more it is unconsciously longed for.

So do not be disheartened. The 'big picture' is in place. The plan of Love continues on. It cannot be otherwise, for Love begets love. It may take a while for humans to realize this, but, as we say, there's no hurry.

You are held in the love of the Beloved, every moment of your existence. Your life is limited not only to the body, to *this* life. The life in which you participate, in which you have your being, is the life of Spirit, of the eternal, ever-present One. Your life is protected, and guided, in a way that is difficult to describe in words. Your 'work' here, which is the same as your learning, is unique. No other embodied spirit has exactly your lessons. A mix of pleasure and pain is the human condition.

This is the Path—to be a compassionate witnessing presence to your life as it unfolds. You have some control over events, but not complete control. The lesson is always to live life from the stance of love—first for yourself. If you come from self-hatred and self-criticism, you simply step in place. No harm done, but no waking up either. The lessons appear as many times as your spirit requires. And there is no judgment here.

What all created beings share in common is the journey toward Love—toward releasing every thing, every desire, any goal that prevents you from living in the awareness of your destiny toward the trajectory of Love. There is no other reason to exist, to be here in this place of duality, where you have as many opportunities as you need to learn about what love is not; about all the myriad opposites of love that allow this one Love to shine in bold relief.

We understand, the not-loves are uncomfortable—they

cause you to be, or rather, you allow them to make you sad, discouraged, disappointed, angry, especially righteously angry. And, each serves a purpose. Every opposite of love points your spirit toward the realization that Love is the only reality, the Love in whose presence these uncomfortable lessons come and then go. You forget, and another, a different one, a variation on the theme of forgetting appears. And then you remember again, or not, because remembering is always a choice. The Universe is generous and patient (we might even suggest long-suffering) because you have as many opportunities, as many lifetimes as it takes, to consciously live in the presence of this Love.

Of course, this stance doesn't make sense to your mind, this mind that has evolved throughout the history of humankind to work mightily to avoid suffering. We invite you to side-step around this avoidance of suffering to an ancient intuitive knowing that is embedded in your eternal being. This place of knowing has had the benefit of much trial and error. It knows how to help your life flow effortlessly toward your good. Your personality, with all its needs, desires and opinions, has the ability to gently step aside; to allow this old knowing of Love's reality to reveal a way that is free from struggle and suffering—that simply and elegantly is. The paradox is that you can't arrive at this place by hard work. Life on the Path is about letting go of all your agendas. It is choosing to live in the presence of Love.

LOVING YOURSELF

Divine Love is cosmic, but also personal and specific. How can the energy that created the Universe love you personally? Because the pantheists are right—God is in everything. God really *is* you, as well as cosmic Creator. When you remember the Love that flows within you, it becomes possible to love yourself. How can you not fall in love with Love?

Love begins with self-love, and self-love is nurtured when children are loved unconditionally. Not spoiled or pampered, but cherished and valued because they exist, because they are concrete expressions of Divinity. They are pure precisely because they don't know it. Their purity and innocence is a reminder of Love embodied. Think of all the expressions of this Love that become confused or forgotten as children learn to distrust themselves, or fear for their physical survival because they lack basic care. Some have no parents or loving care givers to remind them how precious they are.

No matter your beginnings in this lifetime, love yourself in the way Spirit loves you, simply because you are. You may have been taught that you *should* love God. What the Sunday school teachers forgot to tell you is that loving God is the same as loving yourself. You are in a body to learn to love your own unique self. When you recognize who you are—an expression in time of Divinity—there can be no other choice than to love yourself. Yet this truth is forgotten more often than it is remembered, even by those on the Path.

It's a challenge to recognize yourself as sharing in Divinity while you're in a body. There are so many distractions pulling you away from the awareness of your Divine Self. Confusion comes when you try to reconcile your Divinity with the messiness and faults of the human personality. Your personality has a unique collaboration with the soul to which it is joined. It both informs the soul and learns from it, and it's always the perfect vehicle for the lessons you need to learn. This is as true for the most disturbed personalities as for those who are perceived as emotionally healthy. The plan is one of perfection, in spite of apparent imperfection.

The more you are able to see yourself as Love in your essence, the more imperfections of personality can fall away. Whenever you are enticed to act in ways that are less than who you are, remind yourself of your inner God-self. This practice of remembering who you are will not make you egocentric. You are here to learn first to love yourself, then to be Love's vehicle to others. Loving yourself allows you to extend this love to others and to remember who *they* are as well. Taking care of yourself is the most selfless thing you can do. You are able to love others only to the degree that you love and accept yourself. Meeting your own needs first allows you to be generous in a way that would otherwise be impossible.

Until now, humans have barely dared to believe the commandment to love others as you love yourself. As children, many of you were taught that your human nature is intrinsically flawed, so it made sense to mistrust yourselves. Such distortion of the truth can never ultimately be successful, but its subtle aftereffects can linger on to confuse you and catch your heart wisdom off guard. Now you can replace this old belief by practicing a new habit of heart and mind. When you act from a place of self love, you begin to claim your power. If you practice love of self first, the outcomes may astonish you.

You have an inherent right to be here. Love wants more for you than you can ever dream of wanting for yourself. You are a necessary part of creation. Without you, creation would be incomplete. When you claim this birthright, you open your heart to the boundless love of the Universe. When you know that you are a loved child of Spirit, you can open your heart fully to yourself. You can look inside to discover who you are. Then you may ask the questions: Who am I in my essence? Where have I come from? What is my eternal destination? In a mysterious way, the journey *is* the destination. The Path opens under your feet as you step out.

You are here for heart reasons, so it makes sense that your learning involves lessons of the heart. These lessons are for your expansion; they are not designed to make your life difficult. Nevertheless, expansion requires stretching, and stretching can be uncomfortable, even painful. But the pain is temporary, and by the next day your spiritual muscles will be recovering nicely, ready for the next challenge.

Clarity is your ally in this new way of living. You can reach a state of clear mind and heart by remembering to breathe in a conscious way when fear tries to lure you in to all the scary circus sideshows. When you return to your quiet center where truth lies, such distractions can be put aside more easily. Clarity is a habit to cultivate in the midst of busyness, even conflict, so that these heart lessons can become integrated with your mind, emotions and intuition.

When something seems to be impeding the flow of love, return to the self—honor it, get to know it, forgive it; most importantly, send it love. As you love and heal your wounded heart, this love naturally moves outward to others and the world. This is how the work of Spirit gets accomplished on the earth. Love for the world begins with awareness and appreciation of the Self within the self.

How do I deal with persons in my life who are difficult, angry and manipulative?

What is the loving thing to do for yourself and for others in each circumstance? Do these goals seem in conflict with each other? Is it possible to do the loving thing for another if it's unloving for you? Is it possible to love someone else while hating yourself? Is it selfish to do the loving thing for you? In other words, is it loving to set clear boundaries for yourself and others?

You can love another only to the extent that you love and honor yourself. If you dishonor yourself, this radiates out to those you love. Remember that you are a manifestation of the Creator's love. When you understand that your essence is Love, (how easy it is to see that a beloved child is Love) you can act with confidence from your heart space. Actions that flow from love can never be wrong. They may challenge you, but they have a sense of rightness about them that's good for everyone concerned. When you become afraid or doubt your course, go back to love. Ask yourself:

how can I be a manifestation of Love in this situation? This is the only test worth applying.

LOVING OTHERS

Human love honors and remembers the Source of all love. It's but a faint reflection of Spirit's love for creation, an opportunity to give and receive what is present in the hearts of all humans. The desire to love and be loved unconditionally is a memory of your Divine heritage. Spirit is Love poured out without measure to all creatures simply because they exist.

You can be trained to worship an aloof deity out of fear, but you learn about God's love best through love expressed for each other. When you love, you offer back to Divinity the love that is both yours and the Creator's. Spirit doesn't need your love, but desires it in the way that *you* long to be loved.

You can never be separated from the love energy of creation. You are *in* Love, a part of Love—it's impossible for you to be out of love. What does this matter, you may ask, when you feel cut off from the love of an earthly beloved?

It matters, because then you have an opportunity to remind yourself that these events are blips on the screen of eternity, little swells on the sea of Love. You can't escape from Love; you can't be left or leave someone and be out of love. You may not feel the comfort of a specific relationship, but all is still well. Your energetic heart space exists to learn, expand and forgive. The Beloved pursues you through time to eternity. Love is with you in all your adventures, in your happiness *and* your heartbreak.

Love is the driving force of the Universe. It is reflected in the human need to participate in the intense drive to intimacy. Humans are untidy gifts to one another—imperfect bodies, complex emotions, histories of hurting and being hurt. When you accept the gift of another's love, you accept this simmering stew of perfection and imperfection, of limitation and possibility.

In any loving relationship you implicitly accept the eventual loss of your beloved. It means that you are willing to love someone enough to suffer the pain of loss. But this is different from losing the love. Love is never lost. Death has no dominion over it. That human beings are willing to love in the abyss of the unknown speaks to their faith and generosity.

Love creates itself in an exchange of vulnerability, freely given and freely received. True love happens when all aspects of you flow and support each other. When it does, there is celebration throughout the Universe. If you suspect that we exaggerate, it is because you don't yet understand the power of love.

The love we speak of is beyond sex and yet can include it as a vehicle of expression, just as an automobile is not the trip, but the vehicle that allows the exploration. You polish your cars and keep them tuned up; some of you even profess to love them. But even the most avid aficionados know their cars are simply the *means* to get to the ocean or the city, and the journey is often the best part.

The act of making love expresses in a personal way the web of Love that you are all part of. It carries with it special responsibilities and challenges as well as joys. Sex without deep feeling diminishes both persons involved. Until recently, naïve experimentation of this kind carried with it no serious threat to the body, but in these times, the risks of sex pursued carelessly have dramatically increased. Now is a time in human evolution to develop a special reverence for sexuality. The current necessity for caution is in reality a gift.

Sometimes things which pass for love are more like self-indulgence, lust or neediness. Even primitive expressions of love are dim reflections of higher human love—awkward rehearsals for the 'real thing.' The reason all humans have come to this place of duality is to explore the nature of love.

The quality of heart and soul that accompanies conscious lovemaking is satisfying in a complete way. This total expression of loving and being loved on the physical plane is like a preview of coming attractions; it's a reminder of what Love is all about. This kind of love is designed for everybody—the young and the old, the farmer and the physicist. We hope you will make more and more love, but love of the highest quality, the kind that makes the heart and body soar. Love in an orgy of giving and receiving—tenderly, passionately, humorously, with your bodies, minds, hearts and souls—this is the journey designed by you from eternity.

There is always a soul reason for a relationship. It is never mere chance. Its presence is a reminder to trust your soul's journey. Every experience points toward your ultimate return to Oneness. When a loving partner comes into your life, remember that he or she has been present to your soul from eternity. As your personalities come together, your souls rejoice and can appreciate all the circuitous turnings that brought you to this meeting.

Love your own dear self first in any relationship. This love is then reflected outward in a way that feeds the lover and the loved one—a circle of giving and receiving. Loving another with compassion in the midst of your shared imperfections is the safest, most grounded place to be. The adventures you have along the way are journeys to a more intimate connection with the Source of all love. From a place of self-love, there is no fear of abandonment, simply an awareness of participating in this love-force, of allowing yourself to be moved by it.

There is never a reason to fear love or its expression, but sometimes, when love shows up, fear follows, whispering all the 'what-ifs.' The personality starts to hang on for dear life and attach itself to outcomes. It is afraid that love will fail. It is fear that may seek to take control of love. But love is about giving up control. Love is about giving, about pouring yourself out, about letting go of the worry that you may not receive. In love's presence, giving and receiving cease to have meaning because they are so equally present and confluent.

If you have a partner who causes you great pain, we do not say that she is replaceable, for each soul is unique and has a special place in your life. It may be time, however, to let her go as lovingly as you are able. Don't tie her to you with ropes of hatred and resentment. Allow her to move to her next assignment, and wish her well.

Love cannot fail, but it can complete itself in ways that the heart and mind would not choose. If your heart is open, love cannot harm you. Your heart can break again and again, but if through it all you remain open to Love's leadings, you are infinitely safe. To be open to love in sweet vulnerability is the safest stance a human being can take.

Taking time to be alone is good preparation for a strong and balanced partnership; it allows growing space for the soul. Take the time you need to get to know yourself. Remember that you are loved by the part of you that shares in Divinity. This love enables you to reach out to others from a place of fullness. The clearer your inner life, the more this clarity will be reflected in your relationships. As within, so without.

When you are without a partner, know that you are whole and complete in yourself. Cultivate a fullness of grace, which is a kind of spiritual poise, and love will simply go where it goes. We invite you to give up the struggle for love because you are *in* Love. Nothing can separate you from it.

Spirit knows your intimate longings. If you have asked for a partner, trust that if it is for your highest good, one will appear. Visualize this person in your life and enjoy the preparations. And don't limit the Universe by your anxious striving. That's what worry does—it blocks the flow of joy that is waiting.

LOVING WITH AN OPEN HEART

Your lessons are all ways to the Love beyond love. Human love, wonderful as it can sometimes be, is but a rehearsal for the real thing. Spirit loves you in a way no human ever could. Spirit wants more for you than you could ever wish for yourself. The key is to keep your heart open in the midst of every circumstance that would persuade you to shut down. This kind of vulnerability is different from naïveté or lack of discernment. It is rather a choice to be open to Love's leading. And to acknowledge that *you* are part of Love, indivisible from it and of its essence; that without you, Love would be incomplete.

Love is inside you, not out there somewhere. Love is you, and everyone else. Love is every breath you take, every song you sing, every step you dance. And when the breathing and singing and dancing are done here, the party moves on. The music doesn't stop—ever. You can cover your ears, so you hear no melodies, but the dance goes on.

When you are touched by love, it's easy to open your

heart in return. When love appears to have gone missing, it's challenging to open your heart to the void. But emptiness is part of the illusion. In reality the void is fertile, full of potential. You may ask, will love disappoint me again? Will it be worth the risk? Is it too late? A willingness to sit in the heart of unknowing is the epitome of trust. Embrace the unknown, trust its place and its time in your life. Your yearning, your loneliness, even your fears are part of the plan.

Desires are not present in your life to frustrate or dishearten you. They are reminders of the Love that surrounds you now and always. Desires point your heart toward the trajectory of Love. They remind you to keep your heart open when there is no rational reason for doing so.

Sometimes your attempts at loving are rejected. Don't spend a moment worrying about such apparent failures. Love can never fail. It is not your business whether or not it is accepted. Your business is to live with an open heart.

You will meet people who are afraid to live this way. Learning to live with the consequences of a closed heart is *their* lesson. You can love them and wish to change them, but each soul has the key to open its own heart. The timing of when this happens with each person is perfect, even though what you see may look like failure.

Keeping your heart open teaches you the difference between love and dependence. You can love completely and learn when it's appropriate to say no. Your heart can be open even as you set clear boundaries for yourself and others.

What *is* love doing in your life these days? Is love the energy you count on, that you consult as your guide? Or is your collaborator fear? We harp on fear until you're sick of hearing about it, because when you take off fear's mask, you'll find Love waiting. Not the sentimental, 'happily ever after' kind, but the Love that is cosmic, part of you and everyone. You are Love, your friends are Love, your children are Love, your enemies are Love. You can't fall out of it, because then you would cease to exist.

To learn the triumph of love over fear is the quintessential human lesson. Love on the earth plane can never be completely selfless, but that remains the goal. Love for love's sake, for the pure joy of loving. If you are at the place where you and your beloved can love with open hearts, then the love you make together will be God-like, of Spirit as well as flesh. If your love is mixed with fear and ambivalence, it will be full of conflicting messages. Don't berate yourself if your love is not reciprocated. Even if your partner is in fear, *your* business is to love with an open heart.

There are relationships that are for a limited time only. Humans often partner when they are unformed in their development. Because persons live longer and there is more social choice now, these immature liaisons may not survive the maturation of one or both partners. There may come an appropriate time to move on. When this happens, look for the opportunity to complete the relationship in a loving way. Then, the necessary transitions can be made in a context of compassion and sensitivity for all those affected by these endings.

Or you may sense your heart suggesting that this is a time to stay and learn love's lessons in *this* relationship. The test to apply is: what is the loving response for *you*? If you put yourself second, the lesson cannot reveal itself. The goal is always to uncover who you are—Love distilled in a soul and manifested on the earth as a spiritually conscious person. How can you best do this? Where? In whose company? Remember, the criterion is always, 'What would Love do?' Let *this* be your guide, and life's decisions will become simple. Not necessarily easy, but clear decisions that feel right in your body and your spirit.

How can I work through my feelings of possessiveness toward my partner? I am always afraid I will lose her.

When you love someone very much, the fear of loss often stands there beside the love. You can never possess anyone in this creation, because you are all manifestations of the One. If the veil dropped away, you would see that you are all in this eternal web of Love together.

It's always a challenge to love open-heartedly, without possessiveness. Loving someone means being willing to give that person away, because only in loving lightly can you really love at all. What is yours is yours for eternity and can never be taken from you—not by separation or death. Those you love are safe with you always, and now is part of that always. Those who serve your highest purpose will remain. Nothing is ever lost to you that you truly need.

The good news is that you can't be abandoned by Love. If you're tempted to believe that because someone no longer loves you, you are therefore unlovable, you give away your power and sense of self to another whose attention has strayed elsewhere. When you remember the Love in your heart, then other loves in your life enrich your own love. Fear of abandonment is not your enemy. Let it walk beside you a while. Notice what it's made up of—projections into a future that might not happen as you imagine, liberal doses of judgment, smaller doses of perfectionism.

When fear of abandonment comes up, don't try to reason with it. Instead, take it gently by the hand into the heart of your own love. You can never be separated from *this* love, because it is who you are. You can, however, by forgetting who you are, experience separation from yourself and from the Source of Love of which you are an intrinsic part. The experience then *feels like* abandonment, when in reality you are abandoning yourself. Sometimes paths intersect only for awhile, and when you must continue on without the presence of a beloved, the plan is no less perfect for you.

My father's strokes have changed his personality. He's become difficult and angry. How can I keep my heart open to him?

Your father's anger comes from grief and fear. Standing in the way of his anger is like staying in the sun knowing it will burn your skin. In the hot sun, self-love decrees that you cover up and wear a hat. If you ignore these commonsense precautions, you invite a painful sunburn. This doesn't mean that you hate the sunlight. It means that under certain conditions you have to protect yourself from its harmful rays. So it is with your father.

He has a choice about how to deal with these painful losses in his life. You can't force him to agree about what you think would be best for him. Perhaps his pain and resistance is a necessary part of *his* soul journey. *Your* task is to maintain your compassion, sometimes from a distance, both physically and, especially, emotionally. You need to honor your boundaries, to finally be an adult in relation to your parent. As long as you play the anxious child trying to placate and please, you allow this pattern to continue in a way that's destructive to both of you. One of you needs to change the rules, and it's much more likely to be you. Adult love sometimes says "No." or "All right, do it your way." It recognizes that your father has a right to make choices, even risky ones.

Each incarnated soul finds a way to cope with the end of physical life. For some, the force of habit and old conditioning makes this time one of great fear. But fear is a choice, and however painful it may be to look at, perhaps it is necessary for some soul reason. Let go of expectations and 'results.' Neither judge your father's anger and resistance nor indulge it. The schoolroom is sometimes a messy place.

9

Living With Your Guides

Love is the entire content of our
curriculum—and of yours.

Many humans have been working for psycho-
logical and spiritual growth, for peace and
justice, and for the preservation of the planet.
The accumulation of this high intention is evoking the
collaboration of beings like us. The veil is thinner these
days, as more people push past the illusion of matter. Our
mission is to support the personal and planetary turning

toward the Light.

When you join this collaborative effort toward higher evolution, you have access to a new level of knowing and high functioning. This new way of living in the flow of universal energy may seem to happen without your conscious consent, but it is always an agreement with your soul. Your awareness can expand even while you're sleeping, or while you're attending to other business. Welcome these intimations that you are more than your body.

Your spirit helpers are in your life to light it, especially the shadowy places. These dark places continue to become uncovered as you seek the Light. You may think, therefore, that you are regressing. When the Light shines on your shadows, it's for the purpose of bringing truth and love to these places.

Conscious contact with the world of spiritual guides is not a matter of worthiness, it's a gift from the Beloved. As you seek connection to higher wisdom, we can be used as a window into greater reality. Humans on the earth plane aren't cast adrift without resources. We, and others like us, are your spiritual supplies. We are present when our help is known and acknowledged and when we're completely unknown and unacknowledged. When you choose to incarnate, our help is a given.

The perceived separation between you and your guides is an illusion. The world of form, by the density of its nature, resists the world of formlessness. It is the human condition and dilemma. But it's possible to part the veil into formlessness.

WHY WE ARE HERE

Our purpose is to share what we're learning in our state of existence. The truths we learn are the same as those *you* learn through the experience of living in your world. In *this* realm of being, however, the distractions are fewer. Spirit teachers are more readily available to us. Materiality is not a distraction. Things, money, the beauty of the natural world and human love are all part of living life on the earth. They also filter reality. In this era, many souls are going past earthly distortions and distractions.

Humans perceive reality as though looking through a kaleidoscope. Entrancing, but not exactly accurate. We remind you that there is more than eyes can see, ears can hear and arms can hold. We don't say this to criticize the seeing and hearing and holding. They are appropriate, good, even necessary. *And* there is *more*.

On the earth plane, the more is a mystery. It remains veiled, whispered about, thought about much more than most would acknowledge. But your spirit knows. It remembers; it has never forgotten why it is here. These 'intimations of immortality' continue to knock gently at your door, but awareness of the ineffable doesn't come barging in—well, almost never! No matter how much happiness and fulfillment there is in a human life, there is always a sense that something is missing that the soul longs for. This yearning is for union with the indescribable heart of Being. Humans seek a return to the Oneness of which we are all a part—that is our common heritage. Even though the unknown can easily become a source of fear, *this* reunion is not to be feared.

We are here to declare that this Essence of Being can be known on the earth plane, this One who holds all souls in existence because of His/Her passionate longing for reunion. The path within that leads toward Oneness unfolds as it is traveled. Although this journey must be undertaken alone, it is never a lonely one. Companionship on the Path is a given. Souls recognize one another, sometimes at first glance, and sometimes in spite of the disguises of bodies and personalities.

COMMUNICATING WITH YOUR GUIDES

In the midst of the busiest life, there is a sacred place of listening. Into this space of silence comes guidance that can make life both simple and rich. Our favorite way to communicate is through intuition. A second way is to facilitate bringing together those on the Path. Some of these contacts are fleeting, others long term. There is always special joy and a sense of recognition when such soulmates meet. The ability to recognize one another is a function of your developing intuition. A third way is through our collaboration with humans who are becoming more conscious.

Everyone comes into this life with spirit helpers. These guiding energies often change throughout a lifetime, but no one walks unaided on the earth. Life is not meant to be lived alone, and it isn't, even by the most isolated human personality. Loving energy surrounds everyone at every moment. If you could see the abundance of help that's available to you, your lives and the world would change dramatically. But whether you are aware or unaware of them, your guides remain your ever-present companions and helpers. The notion of guardian angels is not Victorian sentimentality. Humans have had hints of this other-worldly protection throughout history and in all cultures.

You don't have to be limited by the physical. The world of spirit hovers close. These spiritual energies often remain silent until you're ready to explore the domain of spirit. And sometimes, there is an unexpected opening, often in the midst of a crisis, but these opportunities have always been prepared and invited in by the soul.

You are in the thick of this world of spirit—surrounded by energy, by beings no longer in bodies, by beings who've never taken form, by layers of light and energy. This is the natural state of humans. The evidence of the senses is so pervasive that it's hard to remember that you are a being of light in the presence of other light beings.

It's always prudent to ask for protection when consciously communicating with the world of spirit. You don't want to waste time on any guidance that comes from other than the highest sources. *Ask for energy only of the highest and visualize yourself surrounded by Light.* This may seem magical, but if these two simple things are done, less highly evolved beings on the astral plane cannot have access to your consciousness.

It may be challenging for you to listen to your guides without allowing any intruding thoughts of your own. But never follow any of our teachings like some spiritual automaton. The mind is present as a censor and your spirit is present as a monitor of truth and integrity. It's always wise to check out the validity of our words in your heart. If what we say rings true for you, you confirm your own deep knowing.

As more souls sense that their lives are a joyous collaboration with their guides and teachers, they cannot help but 'lighten up.' In order for higher guidance to come in, your spirit has to agree to the process, even when your personality may not even know of your soul's wish for this connection. We don't meet with you unless on some level we're invited, although sometimes we knock gently on the door of your consciousness. If you want more contact with us, ask. An intention to be aware of our presence is always honored.

A word to the doubters: if you believe that contact with the world of spirit is impossible, then life will back up your belief at every turn. It's not necessary to persuade anyone of our existence. Our guidance will find its way to those who are open to it.

We know what we say often sounds naïvely optimistic. The good news is that life is sustained by a power of Love both cosmic and personal. In the midst of all that would appear to be its antithesis, we remind you that reality is Love. This is not something we can prove, but neither will we dilute the message so that it's more readily accepted. As we remind our collaborator ever so gently, her belief or lack of it has no power to affect the nature of reality!

We're around to shake things up, to upset the status quo. We expect what we share to be controversial, because what we say doesn't make sense to human logic as it works in most lives. We invite you to suspend your disbelief. Our role is to assist in lighting the Path for our brothers and sisters on the earth plane.

Remember that our message is not only about Light; it's about the quality of *lightness*, which enables you to live your life much more comfortably. If you approach our words with an overly serious attitude, the insights may elude you. Spirit is lighthearted and invites you to enjoy the journey.

Love is the entire content of our curriculum—and of yours.

10

The Path

*In the eternal present and Presence,
the Path unfolds under your feet as you step out.*

*There is more to the story of Bob, my friend, the pilot. He
joined the Air Force for one reason only: he loved to fly. This
was at a time when he and his colleagues were testing a fighter
jet that was seriously flawed. Several of his friends had been
killed in this craft, as suddenly it would stall at high altitudes
and plummet earthward.*

As part of his assignment in Germany, he began to fly

helicopters on civilian rescue missions. He wrote that this was the really important work. On what I imagine was a beautiful day in early winter, he was making a routine test flight over the German countryside when his jet stalled. He called in to the base. They screamed: "Eject! Eject!" But he explained that the trajectory his disabled plane might take on its own could cause it to land on an elementary school. He replied only, "I'm staying with the plane."

You are not only *on* the Path, you create the Path and make it happen. It becomes real as you step out in what you may perceive to be the dark. The Path changes as you change. You encounter it differently as you learn, but it is your companion on your journey to the Light. It is impossible to be off the Path. Side trips, yes. Vacations, of course. A little wandering in the wilderness? That's all right too, because in one sense, there's no hurry.

Embrace your Path even when you don't know where it's leading. You have an opportunity in the midst of the unknown to step forth trusting that the Universe is benign.

If you knew for sure, there would be no need for faith. Acting in the face of the unknown hones your courage and your compassion.

No one is certain—even those who proclaim to be most loudly. When you incarnate, you 'see through a glass darkly.' It's the game everyone agrees to play. But when you *consciously* play the game, you might say: "I know the game. I step out in faith as the way is revealed to me. Sometimes I guess right, but often, my ideas about what to do, where to go and with whom, are off track. No matter. No experience is ever wasted. Hindsight always shows this to me clearly." A rule of the game, however, is not to allow hindsight to become a judge. Simply notice what succeeded and what didn't.

Walk the Path as prepared as it's prudent to be—with some supplies for the journey, but not too many. Keep your eyes on the Path, but also look around so that you can enjoy the sights along the way. Trust that your feet know what to do—that it's not necessary to look down at every step for fear of stumbling. This means occasionally you'll trip and fall or get your feet wet, but you're resilient, and the Self beyond your personality knows that the journey cannot fail.

Don't worry so much about your purpose. Purpose is found in small things as well as in a grand plan. Trust your life more. If the guillotine were about to do its work, you would be in no danger. And what about the things left undone at the end of this lifetime? All we can say is—to be continued.

As for uncertainty—observe it, embrace it, be it. Accepting the not yet known has great power. You really don't have to figure everything out. Mind is an ally, but not your master. You have more resources than your mind. Serendipitous events, books that fall into your hands, friends, loved ones, intuition that nudges, the chance encounter, the melody that soars, the beauty of the natural world—all are guides on the Path.

Allow your life to unfold as you step into the unknown. Each footfall is protected as it touches the ground. The Path is not walked in darkness—rather as in a morning mist when the light is all around you but the Path isn't yet discernible. When you embrace this diffused light you more easily come into clear light.

The Path

On the Path, life becomes simple. You have control of this quality of simplicity even in the midst of the busiest life. Simplifying your life may make it more beautiful. Simplicity is space, silence, elegance. It allows the environment to help center the soul for the important work of Spirit. This doesn't mean you must sleep on a straw mat in a cold hut, or sleep alone. It means choosing things and persons to take along with you on the journey that speak to your heart. Your heart wisdom is older than the body. Check in when there is a decision to be made.

To be kin in the old sense means to belong to the same family or tribe. When you begin to accept as kin those whose hearts are open to the inner life and whose lives meet yours in trust and love, this allows even the most solitary among you a new kind of family—the community of those on the Path. When you trust your intuition to guide you, it becomes increasingly easy to discern these souls. The exciting truth is that those on the Path of conscious intention are drawn strongly to one another. Don't be surprised that you find more and more fellow pilgrims in unlikely places.

The availability of this kind of companionship is not some metaphysical notion. You are never alone in the pursuit of your spiritual growth. Like attracts like, and light attracts light. Those with similar energy and intention are naturally drawn into the orbit of each others' light. This is how the law of attraction works.

These new kin, these seekers on the Path, are gifts of Spirit. They are in your life—some briefly, some long term—for your mutual support and delight. When you live your life in alignment with your highest purpose, you will find like-minded souls to share the journey. Sometimes these spiritual companions are writers whose books you discover, who share their ideas but whose lives do not physically touch yours.

Life on the Path is one of trust, and often one of silence. Most of all, it is a life of listening and learning, of being attentive to subtleties and small things. Listen with an ear cocked to the lessons life offers. Often, this new way of living requires a letting go, but letting go is also a way of letting in—of making room for the new. What is necessary for this letting in is an open heart and a quiet mind. You can train yourself to notice the sense of physical expansiveness in the heart space that prepares the spirit for learning. This way, you willingly live on the rim of mystery. You know by now that life is a mystery—so live it fully, radically, with maximum aliveness.

Your journey is certain to have repercussions in the world. It's not possible to make a commitment to the Path without profound changes happening on the outside as well as the inside. Welcome the changes as a confirmation that the pot is being stirred up. When you walk the Path, you give up the expected and prepare for dynamic change. Sometimes it means being in the stillness of no apparent change. The times of no discernible progress are often the most fertile. One thing is sure: once you are consciously on the soul Path, your life is forever changed.

When you choose the Path, you live in the seen and unseen worlds simultaneously, and the more permeable become the boundaries between them. Living at the same moment in the world of matter and in the world of formlessness is a precious opportunity. Indigenous peoples have always recognized this dual reality and many live their lives from this perspective. In Western societies, people are easily distracted from the inner journey, particularly in large cities. This is why those on the Path like to spend time close to nature. It is easier to listen in such places and to live life in harmony with Spirit.

EACH SOUL'S PLAN

There is really not much you need to know to be successful on the earth journey. It's helpful to travel light—with the possessions that support your journey, but don't weigh it down—and with a light-hearted spirit.

Your soul is on an unerring trajectory back to eternal Oneness. At every moment, you're exactly where you're supposed to be and where your spirit has made a choice to be. This doesn't mean that you're a puppet on a string, manipulated by some cosmic marionette master. *You* are the master, the designer of your life. You've come into a body to reveal yourself fully. You weren't deposited here by some random act of procreation. *You* played a part in coming, and your unique work awaits you.

Each soul is exquisitely guided on its way. No path is worthless and no path is better than another. The timing of outer events, no matter how frustrating, is perfect in its way. Acceptance of this timing sometimes requires courage, even heroism.

All that you discover in your reading, the new people drawn into your life, even things that attract you, are part of the plan to guide you home. And home is as close as your heart. Home *is* your heart. This grand plan is made up of small events, of hours and days and individual tasks—good reasons for going about each day with as much mindfulness as possible. Truth is hidden in the mundane, so honor the small things.

You are here to bring joy to yourself first, *then* to others. If you're in the flow of right energy, this molding into reality of your life purpose will seem like play, not work. Difficulties happen when the personality tries to manipulate the soul's agenda. The requirement, if you wish to live a carefree life, is to surrender to the soul's plan. If struggle is the setting in which you live your life, it's time to renegotiate the contract. *You* choose the context of your life, and a difficult context *can* be changed.

Conscious living has power. A conscious intention to be on the Path allows life to unfold in wonderful and surprising ways. Yet we honor each soul's timing and innate wisdom. The arduous journeys some of you choose are ultimately in the service of lessons to be learned. You can take a break, even drop out of school for awhile. How consistent and committed you are is always your choice, but the lure of this new way of living and learning is imbedded in your soul.

You can prepare the way to live consciously on the Path by living in a monastery for twenty years or several lifetimes, or you can prepare in the midst of an active life in the world. It is not so much that a soul 'deserves' such a breakthrough; it simply becomes time for the next stage of growth. And the soul knows. It knows the journey it is on. It knows in a way that the personality to which it is temporarily joined can never know. As you begin to wake up, you may be surprised by change that has apparently not been sought. This change may be accomplished in the midst of an outer life that seems unaligned with such an intention—when the soul and personality are not yet aware of each other. The 'work' goes on in spite of this split, because desire to be reunited with the Oneness is of the very nature of your spirit. Your connection with Oneness leads you home to your soul and your meandering journeys are part of this plan to ultimately return. You have free will, *and* the will longs for home. As sunflowers turn toward the light, your spirit is impelled toward the inner Light that is at the center of your being.

Turmoil is an indication that you're tired of the way things are; that it's time to move on to the next level of your development. The lesson, again, is to trust your inner knowing. *And* the plan of your soul is perfect even as you have the freedom to act foolishly or wisely. Without free will you would be less than human. Know that you can never be diminished by your own attempts at diminishment—distracted, anxious, over-busy, yes, but harmed or abandoned, never.

Now you have an opportunity to deal with the issue of

yes and no. Even those who consciously say *no* to Spirit are struggling with assent. After you say *yes,* life doesn't necessarily become unmitigated delight. After yes, the deluge, or so the illusion may go. Your yes is a speck of light in the darkness of illusion. Then slowly or sometimes with lightning speed, other pinpricks appear as if the fabric of the night sky is tearing and suddenly vulnerable to light. But the Light never overwhelms you. Your eyes grow accustomed to it, as will those who become attracted to *your* light.

Everyone is on the Path, and the way home is assured. If you're struggling along the way, ask your heart wisdom to guide you through dark and unknown times. The wisdom of the heart is there for each of you to tap into. An intention to know your highest purpose is all that is necessary to reveal it. There is nothing to figure out. This way is not one of abandoning your intellect, refusing to return to your job, waiting for some cosmic bolt to enlighten you. This is a way in which Light informs and illumines the daily tasks and profoundly changes them.

∽⧸

Gifts are waiting to be acknowledged and accepted by everyone in this creation, even those who appear most limited, by your human perception. This is a mystery, because opportunities, abilities, and resources appear so unequally apportioned. But the Universe isn't stingy, nor does it play favorites.

Each soul is a manifestation of the One, and all the myriad personalities with their wisdom and folly are traveling the Path toward Oneness together. This truth unites you in ways that you might prefer not to acknowledge. It makes everyone equal—the bright and the dull, the healthy and the handicapped, the cheerful and the depressed, the kind and the cruel. It reminds you that humans manifest the entire range of experience, from the most evolved to the most depraved.

This stew of life helps you to learn what you're here to learn. The learning gets easy if you let go of your ideas of how your life *should* be. If you view all your adventures as just that, adventures—not tragedy, drama or farce, you become less attached to whatever is happening.

The secret of a happy life is to stay unhooked when dramas beckon and worries dance seductively around you. The glorious truth of being a part of Spirit is that nothing can harm you, not even the most dire circumstance. This is because you are eternal beings—come from, part of, destined by your very nature to return to the One.

A pebble in your shoe is just that; and if you were gunned down today by a terrorist mob—well, it's just that. The you-ness of you moves right along the Path—maybe a little time to catch your breath, take in what's happened, and choose what's next on your journey.

Your brothers and sisters who seem to choose such difficult lives are doing what they're here to do. Addiction, antisocial behavior, even violence may be necessary steps on *their* way home. It's not for anyone to judge. Hold them in love as they walk their painful paths, and, if necessary, get out of their way. You have as many opportunities to learn as you need. When you finally *understand*, you see through the illusion and discover that the Wizard of Oz was just a frightened old man.

Humans long for the good news that it's possible to live life in joy, love and abundance. They want to learn how to do this without struggle. What *is* required is a turning of the spirit toward the Light, making the small everyday decisions in this context. And the timing is always the soul's choice. Does this act or thought move me toward the Light? Or does it distract me or persuade me to believe the world's bad news? Does this thought empower me, or does it evoke my fear? Is this action one that is loving to me first and then to others?

This way of life is about forging new habits of heart and mind. From new heart and new mind will come radical change in your life. Choosing to live your life in joy is a revolutionary decision. However, the mind is a stubborn old machine. All those synapses doing one dance for so long are now being asked to learn another. Daily practice is the key to retraining these connections. Make a meta-decision to live your life in joy. Then the small forgettings, or the automatic return to negative thought patterns lead to gentle modifications along the way.

It's time to try this out. Thinking about it, agreeing with it intellectually, keeps you stepping in place. Again we say, the way to persuade your head that life can be lived in joy is to practice.

THE EVOLUTION OF CONSCIOUSNESS

Your purpose is always and forever the same: to uncover, to peel away all that is not of your essence; to become who you are so clearly that you shine in the world. Every soul who chooses to incarnate knows at some place in consciousness what its purpose and lessons are in this lifetime. Your purpose has been protected from the beginning of beginnings. The uncovering of this purpose and the choices for making it manifest are the ways you participate in Divinity. You get to choose how, when, where, and with whom. When all your faculties—body, intellect, emotions, and talents—are integrated and consonant with your purpose, you trust your intuitive knowing and sense a change in the quality of your life.

There is much to be accomplished in this era for each of

you who is called to the evolution of consciousness on Earth. This is a time of inner preparation, to be acknowledged and welcomed. Consciousness now has the potential to expand quickly. It is why you have agreed to come at this time. We honor your collaboration in this great contemporary work of Spirit: to make Love manifest on earth.

You are here to grow and learn; to change in a palpable way. There is much work to do on the planet in these days. Each of you on the Path is a necessary demonstration of love to those who are confused, or resist the truth that life is a journey—to wholeness, to the *knowing* that Love is all there is. Simple, and yet the personality resists this simplicity; it can't get its mind around such good news. But to overcome this resistance is why every embodied spirit is here—the powerful, the weak, the violent, those who have been violated, the starving ones, the well fed, the creators and the followers. Everyone is here for the same purpose—to let go of everything and everyone in your lives that holds you back; that distracts you from remembering that you are a discrete ensoulment of the Love that holds all creation in existence.

As you put aside ambivalence and negative thoughts, you will begin to understand our teachings. Yes, it can take a long time, because many of you were carefully taught to despise yourselves; to mistrust your own deep trajectories toward truth.

Every negative thought needs to be nipped in the bud; then its roots need to be meticulously removed. New sprouts are easy to remove. Their roots are shallow. But established weeds that begin to flower and sow their seeds— these are stubborn and must be pursued to the ends of their root systems. It's the same with old programming—with negative thoughts about yourself and others; with self-judgment, self-doubt, habits of not thinking yourself good enough; any thing or impulse that says 'no' to your highest aspirations.

The process gets easier the more you practice, the more positive responses become habitual. Gently let the negatives go as you become aware of them. When you forget, forgive yourself, and be grateful for having noticed. Just brush these thoughts from your consciousness without recrimination or guilt. We guarantee—the Path becomes clearer the more you practice.

Now you begin to notice opportunity in everything, in the mundane. Books that 'fall' into your hands do not arrive there by chance—*you* prepare the way by your longing. This is the Path that is everyone's heritage to find, to discover in every person and circumstance. *You* are the one who has the power to wake yourself up. You have the privilege to undo generations of your forbears' fear. This is the work of evolution. It is your *raison d'être,* why you are here now, in this time and place.

We encourage you to go forth boldly, to make mistakes and learn from them in order to make fewer and fewer. Respect the process. Respect its difficulty, and the courage it takes to overcome eons of unconscious behavior and reactivity. This is the beginning of a new era in human development. It is a time to celebrate—a time for hope, a time for love to be uncovered under the detritus of unconscious thoughts.

As you practice a meticulous guarding of your thoughts, your life becomes clear and light, full of energy and clarity of purpose. Life becomes simple as you arrange your time and affairs with wisdom and compassion. Remember, as you become aware of your negative thoughts—of criticism, discouragement, guilt, impatience, judgment, etc., etc.—you are not regressing. First it's the noticing, then sending these thoughts gently on that signals your progress toward the evolution of your consciousness.

We invite you to assent to this process of your evolution—to trust it, to practice discernment about the ways you live in the world, so that your life and everything in it is congruent with your purpose here. This is the test to apply in every situation. Then life becomes simple and sweet, and yes, joyful, because this is your heritage as co-creator with Spirit in these times of profound change and great unfoldment.

Have the rules changed for applying spiritual principles in these times?

There are no hard and fast 'rules' in the Universe. Spirit encourages new learning, new insights in the development of consciousness. The rule book is a human construct—a list of do's and don'ts, rights and wrongs. Spirit trusts its creatures. Rules may have been useful in some stages of your evolution, but they were mostly designed and exploited by those who held power in former times.

It's not that rules no longer apply. It's more that they have been transformed into the wisdom of the heart, into trusting your inner knowing and intuition. Spirit trusts that you now can act from this place of wisdom. It means that you fly by the seat of your spiritual pants, and this requires courage, but also discernment. Will you make 'mistakes' in this new paradigm? Perhaps, but not fatal ones. You see, there can be no fatal, no deadly mistakes. A loving God cannot design Her beloveds that way. So trust these seemingly new rules—they've always been available. It's more that humans haven't dare to step out of their limitations to trust their collaboration with Spirit. Learning to live by these new internal guidelines allows you to collaborate with your deepest, most ancient wisdom.

SIDE TRIPS

Side trips and apparent dead ends aren't what they

appear to be. Every experience can be considered a course correction, in the same way a pilot makes small adjustments to keep a plane on course. Sometimes the adjustments are unpleasant; sometimes they provide new insights or a respite. But on *this* journey, the destination is the center of your being. The journey may appear labyrinthine, and for certain souls, turning away may be necessary in order to experience the relief of turning back again. All of the seemingly unnecessary trips are chosen in order to learn the lessons inherent in them.

Be patient with those who choose to learn the hard way. You can't rescue others' journeys, no matter how much suffering you think you could help them avoid. Their struggles are reminders to let go of *your* struggles, to allow your own journey to be joyous.

When your Path takes unforeseen and uncomfortable turns, you may be tempted to wonder about failure. Have I fallen off the Path, have I been waylaid? Am I lost in the wilderness? These questions are part of the illusion, because you cannot be off the Path. Trust both the integrity of your journey and that you have, in each moment, what is necessary for it. You may take with you what is useful or burdensome, and because of this, your journey may seem more or less of a struggle. But the Path doesn't disappear. In the eternal present and Presence, it unfolds under your feet as you step out.

There are openings in the illusion of apparent closings; there is learning in the presence of ignorance. Nothing is wasted. There is divine economy inherent in every event. The most trivial situations can be used as opportunities to become more awake. You can get lost on a side-trip or welcome it as adventure.

Trips into self-pity and doubt may tempt you to believe you've stepped off the Path. Following paths that are imitations of the Path—those that contain enough truth to be enticing but that ultimately lead to disillusionment—may persuade you that you're lost. You take some trips so that you learn you never need to pass that way again. Some adventures are thinly disguised classrooms. Each soul designs a curriculum for itself. There are required courses, electives, even crash courses in learning a new subject. But the journey's end is never in doubt.

As you take the time to listen to your inner wisdom, you learn to trust it and use it as an aid in both your soul development and in the practicalities of life. Listening in this way prevents unnecessary detours. It facilitates the lessons you are here to learn. Not that there are no lessons on side-trips. Everything that happens ultimately serves the purpose of the soul's learning. The *feelings* evoked on these detours are more important to learn from than the events themselves.

We invite you to remember that your essence is protected from the place of the eternal One. No circumstance or being can separate you from the Love in which you participate, because you are an integral part of this Self that is the Creator. Words are inadequate here. The old God-talk no longer suffices. We use the word Self because God implies a separate being. Self implies one, and the concept of Oneness comes closer to articulating this ineffable reality.

THE PATHS OF POSSIBILITY

Be in the silence of your center with your heart open to

possibility. You can cooperate in the continuum from the potential to the actual or resist it. To live in a condition of pure potential requires a trusting heart. It's a gift of Spirit that empowers you to be in a state of openness to a possibility that reveals no details nor plans. This way, you choose to live in the moment as responsibly as you can, with discernment rather than worry. This new discernment is efficient. It helps you bypass mind's figuring out and goes to the heart of your wisdom. This discernment is not anti-intellectual, but rather wholly intellectual. You bring the skills of mind, heart and spirit to illumine this realm of the not-yet-manifest. The challenge is to be patient with the unknown; to be willing to not even ask a question. Instead be willing, as Rilke says, to *be* the question.

Is communion bread and wine, or the body and blood of the living God? The arguments span the centuries, but your inner knowing asks only one question: am I willing to have my lifeblood mingle with the living force of Creation? If you answer yes, be prepared for amazing changes. The Beloved waits for the moment of assent in every life. This big yes may be made and then forgotten or ignored, but you can never turn back from it. To say yes is why each of you is here. The places in which you perform your rituals or beg pardon for your sins and the altars on which you supplicate your names for Love are as varied as your imaginations can devise. Enroll in whatever courses of study please you. It's all the same university of life. Your intention to enroll is all that's required. In the seeking is the finding. Your graduation is assured from eternity to eternity.

In these times, many are looking for alternatives to the organized religions that no longer seem relevant in their lives. Once you are on the Path, you are a conscious child of Spirit. The symbols you love and the rituals you observe are a personal preference. Is lighting candles superstition? Light attracts light, and intention is everything. Are statues idols? They can be, or they can be reminders to the senses of Spirit, and of masters who lighted the way in the past. Is God in the tabernacle on the altar? Yes, and no less so everywhere, and in everyone.

Truth expands with your capacity to be open. It's not so

much that the dogma you once believed you now recognize as fiction; it's more that what you used to believe contains pieces of a larger truth. You become more aware of the big picture, where you fit into the whole.

There are many paths to truth. Don't be overly concerned about which path to choose. More important is faithfulness to the intention of being on the Path. It is belief that makes a specific way true for you, more than the intrinsic worth of a particular theology. The contemporary seeking and desire for something more is of Spirit, and the marketplace is full of magical mystery tours and cures. Some of it is immature, and some is an expression of the Path. How do you find your way through the bazaar of New Age nostrums? Try out what attracts you, but not like a child who stuffs himself with cotton candy and then gets sick on the Ferris wheel. Check out the validity of what you read and experience. This is the time for a return to the integrity of the heart and the autonomy of each person, but it's not a time to reject all teachers or established paths. Some of you will choose one teacher and some another, and both may be equally wise. The

Universe is generous. The paths are many. The Path is One.

Now that I am developing my spirituality, I am in frequent conflict with my mother who is a fundamentalist. How can I best deal with her?

Being on the Path gives you access to the big spiritual picture. It can also stir up in you the very qualities you criticize in those who are attached to specific religious doctrine. It's surely annoying to experience attitudes of righteousness—and when dogmatism is interpreted as God's will, it's all the more frustrating. Attachment to a codified version of truth is a phase of development to be worked through for those enmeshed in such limitation. They are still giving their power away to an outside authority.

Your mother's attitudes are an opportunity for you to let go of your own righteousness and treat her compassionately. Her attachment to orthodoxy masks a fear of being wrong, and consequently, unsafe. You can be a beacon of light to her by loving the part of her that is perfect, even as you deal with her criticism. If you are able to love her in the midst of her judgment of you, her model of the one correct way may get shaken a little. What is most important is to let go of any agenda to change her.

Everyone is on a path to truth. The difficulty with having it all figured out beforehand is that when truth surprises you, it can't fit into your model. When you are open-hearted, your concept of what truth is changes as you change. Life on the Path allows the parameters of truth and mystery to expand.

It seems to me that Christianity has obscured the meaning of Jesus's teachings. What is the truth in Christ's message?

This being you call Jesus was a clear light and a master teacher. Sometimes a great light behaves in ways that are outside the norms of society and religion, and so threatens the establishment. His clarity was so penetrating that some of his followers thought it necessary to dilute the power of his message by overlaying it with rules and the trappings of ritual. No one needs ritual to be in the presence of Spirit, although rituals can be beautiful and centering. The early church leaders appointed men to be mediators between the truth and ordinary people. But everyone is ordinary *and* extraordinary, and no one needs a hierarchy to interpret truth. Jesus reminds us that the teacher, the seeker and the sought are within. If you are in touch with your inner teacher, then other teachers can clarify and support your internal knowing. When you believe only in outside authority, whether a religion or a guru, you dishonor your own source of wisdom. It's the same as saying, "So and so is Spirit, but I am not Spirit."

The Course in Miracles is a way to get past the historical distortions and return to the authentic message of Jesus. It is a powerful path for many in this time.

EMISSARIES OF SPIRIT

We bring you good news, but our news doesn't depend on a messiah in human form. Each of you who is open to the Light is an emissary of Spirit to those you know and influence. Many light-bearers are on earth now, and never before in human history have they been so called and needed. As you see all around you, this is a time of extremes. Many are stuck in the rigidity of their beliefs and in the darkness of zealotry. Others are breaking out of old orthodoxies to be open to Spirit's leading. Consciousness is expanding, hearts and spirits are opening, and this is just a beginning.

There is nothing to fear in times that seem so fearful. There are losses that we would label as change; transitions out of the body into the fuller presence of Spirit. If you close your heart and resist change, then you experience it as loss. If you flow with the new and leave the old behind as baggage no longer necessary, then the new can become adventure. The key is to let life flow through you—persons, things, places, roles in the world. All are fleeting, but *you* are an eternal being come from the One, never separated through all your journeying, and destined to return to the One. This is your destiny—an everlasting covenant of safety.

Enjoy the experiences of the earth plane and yet remain unattached to them, including the pain. Pain and separation are illusions, so why be attached to pseudo realities when only Love is real. Your assignment is to manifest love—to offer it to the lonely; to send it to those whose hearts are closed by hatred; to share it with your community of compatible spirits.

Your work is to cultivate a habit of loving. Your work may be to send love to a world leader whom you distrust or judge contemptible. (Your judgment helps keep his heart closed.) Your work is to offer love to those who have hurt you, and to those whom you have hurt in turn. Your work is to chip away at everything in you that is not love. This requires attention, so that you remember to change your automatic unloving responses—a kind of 'work,' but more a retraining of your habitual thoughts. New habits take time to acquire, but they're possible. Remember what you know and forget so easily—you are an emissary of Spirit in this time of great transition on the earth.

This new model of reality is yours for the claiming. You have a unique opportunity *now*, to experience that you are co-creators with Spirit. You can choose to see things from your God-nature. As more of you make these choices, your earth experience may transform before your eyes. These transformations will not all be slow. Some will be instantaneous and complete. It's a very exciting time to be on the earth.

The Journey Home

The journey, our beloveds, is home to *you*. This journey is not designed to be a fearsome trip. It is why you have come. You can put it off and pretend it's not time to leave for your next assignment, but the journey remains to be taken whenever you're ready. Spirit doesn't bully or harass. It gently nudges you to remember what you already know. And there is always support on this journey. As you claim your courage and your purpose, companions appear, because everyone is on a unique yet similar journey. Light attracts light, and so you will be comforted.

The details of your life are held in the context of protection. This is a manifestation of divine economy *and* divine generosity. All is well—always. The details are merely details. Sunny days, rainy days—the variety provides a necessary balance. You are never given more to deal with than you can manage. Welcome challenges as confirmation that your spiritual muscles are strong enough for important jobs. Remember to breathe into the task of the moment.

Say yes to it, even when it's not the preference of your personality. Do what you do with gratitude for each moment of opportunity to learn and grow.

All that is ever necessary is that you be fully present to each moment. Simple and difficult. Simple because the present moment is all there is. Difficult because life offers a constant stream of distractions—some pleasant, some scary, some involved with the busyness of daily life. It is useful to remember that while you're busy with life's minutiae, with your tasks, your opinions, your loves, your worries—life slips by, almost without your noticing.

When fear comes up, stop for a moment, and remember—that *this* set of experiences, *this* body is finite. You've been trained, so carefully, to fear finiteness, endings, the death of the body. But endings *always* have another dimension, an opening to another beginning. This is what seems so incredible, because the physical evidence for this continuity of being is sketchy at best. Yes, there are 'intimations of immortality,' but intimations they mostly remain.

This is where faith comes in. Faith is nothing you are

able to pin down or prove with empirical evidence, but it *can* be experienced. This kernel of faith is a gift. It comes unbidden. It can be prayed for, hoped for, the ground can be prepared by spiritual practice, but often it comes unexpectedly. It breaks through your conditioning. There is something inside you that *knows*, that demands to be noticed. This is the true human condition, this noticing that you are more than bodies and histories and striving and suffering. You are here, purposefully, to learn through all your forgetting and stumbling and fearing; to learn through your growing and remembering.

Ultimately, the remembering will prevail. When you fully remember, you know all that is necessary, and this knowing gives meaning to your life. Then you're freed, emancipated, to go on to the next level of learning. This is the divine plan for every sentient being—no exceptions.

All the pain and grief that is experienced on the earth plane is leading inexorably to a more conscious, evolved species. We proclaim this in the midst of poverty, disease and war. The good news is that *everyone* evolves to higher consciousness, eventually. The plan is perfect in the face of all apparent limitation—and the illusion is beginning to crack. The chicks in this new paradigm are picking away at the shell of forgetting. The memory of who you really are is available *now*. Dry your feathers and begin to see with newborn eyes.

Existence is an endless circle of learning, loving, and being loved. *We* continue to learn, the same as you. We remind you of your wisdom, of the teacher who is part of you; that you have everything you need for the journey, and this *is* a journey, even when wholly inward. And we remind you again that you are in no danger, ever. Your journey home is guided and protected. We don't minimize your dilemmas and difficulties, but we suggest that you hold all of your experience lightly. Cultivate a sense of play and lightheartedness as an antidote to all the stress, self-importance and seriousness that permeate this era. A quality of lightness is the most appropriate response to a heavy sense of struggle that many believe to be an inescapable part of life. In the midst of all that would persuade you to be anxious, your assignment is to be lighthearted.

In this era, there is unparalleled opportunity to shine Light into the darkness of confusion and fear. Surround yourself with the protection of this Light. As your choices are guided by it, they are no less your choices. Remember again who you are when you forget; when others forget or choose not to recognize you.

There are guides from many dimensions who are helping at this time of profound unfoldment of human potential. The evolution of humans is not imagination; it's real. And we're here to guide you and others over the rough spots. This awakening to greater consciousness in your species will come with challenges, but not impossible ones. It is our pleasure and our commitment to help in whatever ways we can. All is well, our dear ones. The plan of evolution, which is the plan of Love, is in place.

You are all facets of the Light. You, and we, are light-bearers, yet many still believe in darkness. When Jesus said, "I am the Light of the world," he was revealing his great light to remind others of *their* light. Since the beginning of humankind, many have allowed their light to shine, and this chain of light-bearers continues, a luminous web spiraling into the One. Eventually, our spirits will be one with each other and with the Source in a way that words cannot describe. Words are inadequate to express the reality of this holy, overarching mystery that holds all creatures, everywhere in the cosmos, in Love. When you remember to be present to the awe of this mystery, life begins to make sense. Then you are aware of its context, of your existence and your share in this vast web of Love.

Beginnings and endings follow each other in a spiral, unlike a highway that takes you directly from one place to another. On *this* trip you will meet both familiar faces and friends disguised as strangers. In the process, *you* will be unmasked, this uniqueness of you. This is your purpose—to manifest your participation in Divinity, to make your contribution to the whole, to shine your light first for you, and then as a beacon for others. This is not grandiosity. It is the essence of the human journey.

Do you see how simple the plan is? It's about changing your perception so that you are able to experience what has always been true—you are a creation of Love, destined for union with Love. You have incarnated now to make this reality believable through *you*.

Spirit waits eagerly for you to accept and reciprocate its love. We surround each of you who reads these words with *our* protection and love. We wish you clarity of purpose and an inner calm that reminds you that you aren't lost—you're on the journey home.

About the Scribe

Maureen Kennedy has published Circle Round the Zero (MMB, St. Louis), a collection of play chants and singing games of city children. She is a contributor to the three volume series, Music for Children, Orff Schulwerk, American Edition (Schott Music Corp.). She taught at Wheelock College and was the director of the master's program in Orff Studies at the New England Conservatory of Music. In addition, she was part of a research demonstration team in the Department of Psychiatry, Yale School of Medicine, which studied the impact of socialization on persons with serious and long-term mental illness.

Maureen is currently working on a collection of her poetry. She lives in the hills of western Massachusetts, and is the mother of three adult sons.